The Dynamics of
Effective
Negotiation

Gulf Publishing Company
Book Division
Houston, London, Paris, Tokyo

The Dynamics of
Effective
Negotiation

Donald B. Sparks

to Danna Sue,
who combines charm
with purpose

The Dynamics of Effective Negotiation

Library of Congress Cataloging in Publication Data

Sparks, Donald B.
  The dynamics of effective negotiation.
  Includes index.
  1. Negotiation. I. Title.
BF637.N4S65   658.4   81-24438
ISBN 0-87201-582-3   AACR2

Contents

Foreword

Today, the negotiations process has captured public interest. It is perceived by corporate and public executives as being a pragmatic means of attaining organizational goals. Long before this process became so popular, Don Sparks was helping people develop negotiating skills, using illustrations of appropriate negotiating techniques which produce success. Improperly used, these techniques can result in failure; hence the importance of understanding Don Sparks' general methods and approach when tackling specific negotiating situations.

Applying Sparks' methods to negotiating problems can result in agreements that need not be constantly monitored and reworked, thereby saving much valuable time. The overall approach of this book centers on long-range relationships, with a balanced emphasis on present, competitively sought objectives. A grasp of this book's teachings will help any negotiator achieve maximum effectiveness and greater professionalism.

Jerry P. Clousson, J.D., L.L.M.
Director, Department of Negotiations
American Medical Association

Preface

This book is intended to encourage a systematic approach to negotiations. Negotiation is an attempt to reach an agreement on some issue over which two or more parties disagree.

A systematic approach goes a long way toward attaining three goals. First, it helps resolve more issues successfully, which is done by accomplishing a win/win whenever possible. Second, it increases trust, respect, and commitment between parties that have on-going or repeat negotiations. This means acting in a manner that fosters a long-term relationship valued by both parties. Third, it minimizes the time spent in negotiations by doing them well the first time. This requires producing resolutions that are genuinely sound and that can in fact be implemented.

The Dynamics of Effective Negotiation is unlike other books about negotiations. It demonstrates the merits of conducting negotiations pragmatically as opposed to considering them an art form, and emphasizes the areas experience shows are critical to successful negotiations. The negotiator must prepare for negotiations using a step-by-step method (as opposed to relying fundamentally on experience and knowledge, as is stressed in most books). He must also adopt an *issue* orientation; negotiating "style" is important, but it must assume a position of secondary importance to the issues at hand.

The bulk of current literature on negotiations emphasizes me-versus-you strategies, out-and-out use of gimmicks, and techniques often unsubstantiated by research. This emphasis is misplaced. It leads to reliance on actions that are essentially win/lose oriented. It also denies much of the scientific findings of intergroup psychological research, which describe methods for merging the actions of individuals or groups into productive channels and techniques for reducing unproductive conflicts.

The techniques presented here will help negotiators at all levels of experience. Methods are provided for resolving issues fairly, even when the opponent is challenging with methods geared to one-way resolution. Issue resolution based on the merits of both parties' positions is emphasized. The techniques for this are spelled out. Examples illustrate how the techniques work, and guidelines for when and where to use them are provided.

All the gimmicks known, including intimidation, will shatter like glass when thrown against the rock of win/win negotiations. Agreements forged through win/win negotiations have an extremely high probability of being enacted because issue resolution in win/win negotiations is heavily based on merit—on what should be. This is its major strength. Experience indicates that most people will stick to equitable agreements. Also, win/win negotiations offer the best chance of avoiding residual hostilities which often damage post-agreement follow-through.

The weakness in non-win/win negotiating methods is that issue resolution many times does not occur. Instead, agreements are forced through intimidation, the use of power, or time pressure manipulation. These methods leave the question of issue merit unsettled. The unresolved merit question becomes a latent source of problems, generally arising at the most inconvenient times.

The approaches described are designed for industrial use (when properly modified they can be applied to personal negotiations as well). While the book concentrates on negotiations in the industrialized western countries, it is also useful for international negotiations to varying degrees, based on the amount of cultural similarity to the western countries.

To become fully proficient with the win/win approach, a negotiator must understand and accept four key things (which constitute the main parts of this book):

1. The characteristics of negotiations (Chapters 1-4).
2. The need for disciplined, diligent preparation (Chapters 5-6).
3. The use of common-sense methods for conducting negotiations (Chapter 7-11).
4. The skills required to work effectively with style-oriented opponents (Chapters 12-14).

The terms "negotiator" and "opponent" are used throughout this book to describe the two parties in a negotiation. "Negotiator" denotes the skilled individual utilizing a win/win approach. "Opponent" signifies those people opposing the negotiator; it encompasses many styles and approaches to negotiating. Opponents may, of course, be as skilled as negotiators. There is no implication that they should be underrated. Instead, the intent throughout this book is to learn how to work successfully with others who do not share the win/win approach to negotiating.

Donald B. Sparks
January 1982

Acknowledgments

My appreciation goes to Robert Aldag, III, Contracting Department, Arabian American Oil Company; James Jeffries, Coca-Cola Foods Division, Coca-Cola Company; E. J. Townsend, Jr., General Systems Division, International Business Machines Corporation; and Mrs. Danna W. Sparks for their able assistance in preparation and editing. A note of thanks goes to the several thousand participants in my Negotiating Skills Improvement seminars conducted over the past seven years. These seminars provided the opportunity for synthesizing material into this book. Equally important has been the refinement of my own ideas about negotiating obtained through consulting work with clients.

Part I

The Negotiation Process

CHAPTER 1

Characteristics of the Negotiating Situation

The North Wind and the Sun

The North Wind and the Sun disputed as to which was the most powerful, and agreed that he should be declared the victor who could first strip a wayfaring man of his clothes. The North Wind first tried his power and blew with all his might, but the keener his blasts, the closer the traveler wrapped his cloak around him, until at last, resigning all hope of victory, the Wind called upon the Sun to see what he could do. The Sun suddenly shone out with all his warmth. The traveler no sooner felt his genial rays than he took off one garment after another, and, at last, fairly overcome with heat, undressed and bathed in a stream that lay in his path.

Persuasion is better than force.
Aesop's Fables

The Five Negotiating Characteristics

Negotiating situations can be identified through their five characteristics:

1. An exchange of giving and taking between two parties.
2. The simultaneous existence of restraints and drives, resulting in friction between or discomfort to the parties.

3

3. A reasonably important issue or question, the resolution of which is sought by the parties.
4. The presence of uncertainty.
5. The existence of real or perceived conflict between the positions of the parties.

Exchange

Negotiations characteristically involve an exchange of giving and taking between the negotiator and opponent. Through this exchange, they attempt to reach an agreeable or acceptable conclusion in settling an issue or dispute. The negotiator expects the opponent to move from his original position toward the negotiator's, and vice versa. Some of this movement involves concessions. Some involves goal readjustment. Some results from the difference in concern about the various points in question; i.e., one party may have only one point of prime importance while the other party has three points. The amount of movement determines, in the end, which party got more of its aims.

The exchange presents a special problem for some people who are numerically or volume oriented. They prefer many wins, even though these may be small in importance individually. These people are apt to pass by a major item in exchange for several minor items. Goal congruity in planning for a negotiation helps prevent the negotiator from slipping into a numerical orientation. This congruity keeps the focus on what is being sought and whether or not it is being achieved.

Failure to stick to a quid pro quo philosophy hurts the chances of a negotiator being successful. An opponent who gets a concession without giving one develops an expectation that other concessions are available without cost. He is then surprised at any behavior that is different, such as the negotiator expecting a return concession. There should be no free lunches.

In the win/win approach, the issue being negotiated is highlighted as central. This might be quantitative, such as the amount of service to be given, or the number of items involved, or the price or cost. It might also be a qualitative issue involving company image or industry practice. What is definitely not the concern in win/win negotiations is the personalities of the parties involved. They are left out of the deliberation. Methods for controlling reaction to opponent personalities are discussed in Chapter 6.

Example

A negotiator has two negotiations scheduled. The first involves settling a $1,000,000 claim against his company by a contractor. The amount of money involved, future relations with contractors, and the potential establishment of a practice or position regarding such claims make this an important issue. To negotiate the claim properly, the negotiator would invest the time and energy to deal with its importance. He is going to negotiate at a level commensurate to the issue's importance. The second negotiation involves a maintenance contractor. The contractor selection was dictated by a low-bid policy. The negotiation will concentrate on settling the contractor schedules for when the work will take place. It may also involve the question of how payments are made—lump sum, progress, or a combination of the two. This second negotiation is less important than the claim resolution, both by economic value and by how much the outcome can be influenced. The negotiator spends less time on the second issue.

Guideline: The objective of the skilled negotiator is to negotiate at the level of the issue. Level is defined as the importance of the issue. For major items, more time and effort are required. Every item should not be treated the same.

Friction

The second characteristic of negotiations is that the exchange is uncomfortable, even stressful to the parties. The word negotiate means, in Latin, *neg* for not and *otium* for ease. In a negotiation, one is not at ease until the agreement is made. There are two forces which operate in opposite directions within each party to produce friction.

Restraints operate to retard progress toward resolution and they are generally expressed as questions: What am I going to gain or lose for my side? Is the other party trustworthy? What effect might this agreement have on our competition? *Drives* operate to push progress toward resolution, and they are generally represented as needs: the desire to be cooperative with others; the wish to influence others; and the hope that the deliberation can be brought to a successful conclusion. The intensity of friction caused by these two forces converts into stress felt by each party. How this stress is handled depends on an individual's emotional maturity and self-discipline.

Ways in which negotiators can increase their level of self-discipline are discussed in Chapter 6.

Importance

Negotiations should be reserved for situations requiring serious effort—those for which other methods of conclusion are less suitable. This third characteristic of negotiation raises the question of how a negotiator should allot time to accomplish the tasks necessary. There is a practical way to increase the time available for negotiating, without taking time from other equally important areas. A negotiator must clean off items from his negotiating workload that can be dealt with in other ways. The procedure for this clean off is straightforward:

1. List all items negotiated.
2. Analyze each item based on whatever factors are considered important.
3. Make a disposition for each item: retain, reassign, or relegate it to a set method or procedure.

Figure 1-1 presents a layout for compiling the list, evaluating the relative worth of each item, and making the disposition. It might require one day or several to gather sufficient information. The items

Item	$ Value	Frequency			Hours	$ Importance	Disposition
		D	W	M			
Expedite spare parts contracts	200		1		2	50	Keep
Order office materials	90	2			1		Formulate procedure
Review, renegotiate claims on delay	3000			1	15	2000	Keep
Special price concessions on all large orders	1000		1		?	300	Keep
Check on lead-time revision possibilities	300	1			8	50	Delegate to staff

Figure 1-1. Analyzing where negotiating time is spent. (Source: Sparks Consultants.)

should represent the extent and variety with which the negotiator deals. Once the disposition is made, the amount of negotiating time can remain the same. The focus is redirected to those items that have the potential to produce the best payout for the effort made. Four points should be observed in making the disposition:

1. Frequently recurring items are good targets for control through routine or procedure.
2. Items having multiple uses or potential for increased economic benefit to the organization should receive greater attention.
3. Static items or those with few uses, but still requiring negotiation, are candidates for delegation to subordinates.
4. Some items can be eliminated since they are not really negotiable, not relative to the organization's objectives, or not important. These are usually around because of a negotiator's personal preference.

Time allocation for individual negotiations is part of the planning for those negotiations. The options for gaining more negotiating time are to make it more efficient, or to expand it by reducing other work time or by adding more hours.

Guideline: A disciplined negotiator will review the allocation of his negotiating efforts on a periodic basis.

Uncertainty

The fourth characteristic of negotiations is that there is an inherent uncertainty in them—they require a situational approach. Negotiation is too complex a process to base strategy even mostly on past, proven experiences. Personal experiences shape concepts about negotiations. They lead to telltale habits and predictable patterns. These become liabilities to their host and opportunities for unwarranted advantage to his opponent. Flexibility is what is required. It is best achieved by adopting an issue orientation. This does not mean changing one's personality. It means locking onto the issue, selecting a strategy that is comfortable to use, and adopting tactics fitting one's skills.

Chapter 5 discusses methods that aid in gaining and retaining an issue orientation.

Conflict

The existence of conflict between the positions of the parties is the fifth characteristic of negotiations. While its intensity varies, conflict is an important ingredient in negotiations. Without it, there tends to be little motivation for working hard to find a good solution. Negotiators who are able to distinguish between common disagreement and conflict appreciate the latter's role.

Disagreement is any difference between two parties. However, general disagreement does not result in a collision between those two parties, due to a collision between their goals.

There are three types of conflict: resource, pathway, and value. These types always occur in combination. The negotiator must recognize these types and identify which is dominant in the issue being negotiated. Two types of conflict are somewhat easier to deal with; they lend themselves to quantitative assessment or, at least, to definitions.

In *resource conflict,* mutually exclusive goals are the aim of each party because of limitations on resources—time, money, space, etc. If one party gets its goal, the other cannot, since resources are unavailable for satisfying both goals.

In resource conflict where a win/win approach is attempted, each party strives to gain a victory over the other. The victory is attained through resolution of the issue and is largely based on the merits of the two parties' positions. This contrasts with trying to defeat or suppress the other party, as in win/lose. When the victory under win/win is attained by one party, there is no stigma to the other. The victory may involve only one point out of several. A win/win settlement is not equally favorable to both parties. However, since the conflict has been reduced without personal abuse or intimidation, both parties can support the resolution.

In *pathway conflict,* the dispute centers on how something should be accomplished. The goal is agreed to, but not the way to implement it. An example of pathway conflict that is common in manufacturing companies will help here.

Example

The chief executive announces a drive to increase profit. The suggestion from marketing might be to cut General and Administrative expense. The suggestion from manufacturing might be to increase the length of product runs to minimize set-up expense. Both responses are correct as far as their proponents' views. Where options of approximate equal value exist, the option selected should be the result of negotiation.

In pathway conflict, each party supports achievement of an accepted goal based on concern for its own convenience or position. In reducing pathway conflict, a loss of confidence by one party in the other must be avoided. Again, a win/win attitude which deals with the issue provides the best opportunity for an acceptable resolution, one that will be supported later.

The third type of conflict is the toughest with which to deal. Negotiators need to recognize this kind of conflict quickly. It must be handled differently than the other two kinds, otherwise there is the risk of becoming involved in drawn-out negotiations, often over non-essential or hard-to-define questions. *Value conflict* is often emotionally connected to a commitment or belief which arouses responses that ignore facts. These intense feelings are not changed easily by their holder. The negotiator may not be able to influence them, no matter how skillful.

Example

A contractor for a construction job overseas includes in its proposal that first-class travel and luxury housing be provided for its employees on that job. The contractor states that its policy stipulates these two actions. The customer for whom the work will be done responds that its policy is to furnish tourist travel and economy housing. Travel and housing do not fit directly with work quality or schedule as far as the customer sees it. But the issue is an important one in the context of value conflict: Will contractor personnel feel better enough about first-class travel and luxury housing to do a better job or to complete the work ahead of schedule? What is the benefit to the customer? How is that benefit measured? Perhaps the contractor should pay the extra amount if it matters so much. Is this really the customer's problem? This conflict has more to do with feelings than fact.

When confronted with an issue dominated by value conflict, the negotiator has several handling options. The order in which they should be tried is listed as follows:

1. Let the opponent vent his feelings about the issue. Do not challenge those feelings.
2. Proceed without acknowledgment. This ignores the opponent's basic direction. Sometimes just venting is enough to get him over the hurdle. Break away for a recess to give the opponent time to cool down. He can conveniently resume on a rational note.
3. Seek to identify an issue of approximate equal value and attraction to the opponent that can be substituted for the one causing the value conflict. This is difficult, since it involves a complex psychological transfer. If such an issue is found, it can be given to the opponent at an appropriate time. The chance is then regained to resolve the original issue realistically.
4. Never give in to a value-based position. That almost always leads to larger value-based demands. It is better to abort the negotiation than to fall into and down an endless tube of irrational, unrealistic demands chain-linked by emotion.

Two additional points regarding conflict in general are worth remembering because they constitute a double jeopardy. The longer a conflict exists, the more likely its importance will escalate. Figure 1-2 depicts this change. Furthermore, unresolved conflicts most likely distort the importance of future conflicts. They are intensified. What is true for conflict in general is especially true for conflict in negotiations.

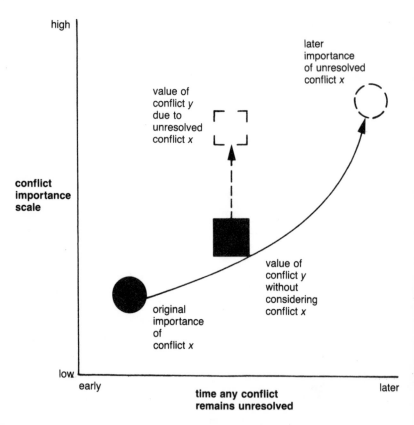

Figure 1-2. The effect of time on the element of conflict importance. (Source: *Games People Play,* E. Berne.)

Guideline: It is best to try to resolve all the issues or to dispose of them by mutual accord. If any are left lying around unresolved, they will pop up at the worst possible time.

In the next chapter the possible outcomes from negotiations are examined.

CHAPTER 2

Negotiating Outcomes

The Two Frogs

Two Frogs dwelt in the same pool. When the pool dried up under the summer's heat, they left it and set out together for another home. As they went along they chanced to pass a deep well, amply supplied with water, and when they saw it, one of the Frogs said to the other, "Let us descend and make our abode in this well; it will furnish us with shelter and food." The other replied with greater caution, "But suppose the water should fail us. How can we get out again from so great a depth?"

Do nothing without regard to the consequences.
Aesop's Fables

All negotiations have an outcome. Each outcome will be viewed as positive or negative. This will be based more on how it was obtained, the methods used, and less on its quality or correctness. There are three positive outcomes:

1. Solution or adjustment
2. Compromise
3. Correction

There are three negative outcomes:

1. Imposition
2. Surrender
3. Stalemate

Positive Outcomes

Solution, compromise, and correction are positive because they produce satisfactory agreements. These agreements are seen by both parties as beneficial and fair.

Solutions

Solutions are rare. They come about when the negotiator and opponent both get all they want. In such cases, the negotiation took place because of requirements or false impressions for its need rather than a conflict. The requirements might be procedural, governmental, etc.

Example

A company requires a contract for all expenditures greater than $10,000. The company wants a technological device from a sole source. Contract negotiation centers on terms and conditions. However, the price is the goal sought by the supplier. The customer is willing to pay, since the device is unavailable elsewhere. Both parties encounter little difficulty in achieving their different major aims.

The solution example could become an adjustment example. The parties might encounter minor differences and have to work through them before resolution. Agreements negotiated by solution or adjustment are almost always carried out successfully.

Compromise

In compromise, the negotiator and opponent each give in on some part of their major and, probably, minor aims. This is done in order to realize closure on other aims. Compromise is a more frequent outcome than solution or adjustment. When one party is giving during compromise, it attempts to minimize its loss. The level of each party's negotiating skills greatly influences the content of compromise outcomes. The result of compromise is that both the negotiator and opponent share in the winning. Usually the sharing is not equal.

Agreements negotiated by compromise have a great chance of being carried out successfully. They require more attention to follow-up than do agreements resulting from solution or adjustment.

Correction

Correction occurs when one party uses invalid or incorrect data as a basis to support its position. This is embarrassing when the other party proves the use of faulty data, unsupportable conclusions, etc. The typical cause of correction is sloppy and undisciplined preparation; sometimes it is a lapse in judgment.

Corrections to one side almost always result in a clear win by the other party. It is a positive outcome because one does it to himself. When a negotiator experiences a correction, he should take at least three actions.

1. Admit the error. Why waste everyone's time trying to argue away what is obvious? Admitting may help build trust with the opponent. Something is salvaged.
2. Limit the correction to the issue under discussion; do not permit its being expanded to other issues. If the negotiator's information is invalid about a specific issue, it does not follow that all of the other information he has is similarly incorrect.
3. Take a recess. This avoids any psychological letdown carrying over to weaken the negotiator's resolve on the next issue. Also,

it takes the edge off the unearned advantage handed the opponent. However, the negotiator should keep in mind that whatever happens just prior to a recess influences the thinking during the recess. The recess permits time to determine whether an error actually occurred or whether mitigating factors exist.

Chapter 5 presents methods that minimize the chance that a negotiator will experience a correction.

Negative Outcomes

The next three outcomes do not resolve the issue, although they may result in an agreement. In brief, the conflict remains. The settlement is very likely to be temporary. However, sometimes a temporary settlement can be better than any of the currently available alternatives.

Imposition

Imposition happens because one party is in a position of almost total power. It can push its way over the other party regardless of the merit of either side's position. The use of intimidating tactics is one form of imposition.

Example
An opponent may threaten legal action over an item in dispute if his demands for a settlement are not met. The negotiator feels the demands being made are excessive. However, he may determine that it is more costly to litigate than to settle. If the opponent demands are met under this circumstance, is the issue really settled? Probably not.

Experience shows that the intimidated party will continually seek means and ways to undo imposed agreements. It will also try to position itself to return the favor, so to speak. Imposition of one's goals through power is a short-sighted way to negotiate. Another form of imposition is the use of time to cause one party to wear out, to submit because of attrition, to weaken because it senses the futility of ever getting its views appreciated, or to be caught in dire need of what the imposing party can provide. Here again, the issue is not resolved based on merit. It is, therefore, still open. Once the time pressure is removed, the party that yielded to it may become resolute in its own demands. In brief, imposition always causes a win/lose outcome, either real or perceived, by at least one of the parties. Along with the dissatisfaction about the agreement, future relations between the parties are damaged.

Counters to imposition tactics are described in Chapter 7.

Surrender

Surrender takes place when one party is persuaded that it will suffer more by getting what it wants than by giving in to the other party. Success is viewed as costing more than the gain. For instance, a supplier might be able to push through a stiff price increase over customer objections in the short run. But the customer will almost surely seek other supply sources if he sees the size of the increase as unjustified. Surrenders sometimes occur because of internal pressure from higher authority within one's own organization.

Example

An important contract for turnkey construction of a large chemical processing plant was being negotiated by a US-based contractor and a foreign government. The customer set the negotiating period for November. When progress was slow, executives of the parent of the contractor—a publicly listed company—pressured the contractor to make concessions. The parent wanted to announce the backlog in its fourth- quarter statement of operations to help its overall performance picture within the investment community. Such research by the foreign government into US business practice paid off.

Generally, surrender results in issue settlements that are unwarranted. As with imposition, surrender leaves the question of issue merit undealt with, the issue unresolved. Surrender, unlike imposition, may avoid harming future relations. But circumstances often arise during agreement implementation that resurrect the issue anyway. What can be learned from reviewing the experiences following imposition and surrender? Just this: If the issue is not settled, it does not often go away. It makes more sense, then, to deal with the issue.

Stalemate

Stalemate occurs when neither party wants to continue toward a settlement, when both adopt fixed, entrenched positions, or when neither party sees any benefit from creating a change that will permit progress toward settlement. Stalemate can result from each party believing it can afford to wait out the other. It is sometimes used to force the negotiation to the next higher level of authority.

When a stalemate is encountered by the negotiator, he should explore options before accepting a total breakdown. These options are listed as follows, in order of the ease with which they can be employed. Selecting an option is based on the negotiator's estimate of which one has the best chance of succeeding.

1. Restate the issue or point in question. This has the purpose of being sure that everyone is thinking of the same thing in the same way. It determines that the stalemate is real. If there is misunderstanding, however, it is cleared up by the restatement. Progress can then resume.
2. Take a recess, then start fresh. Perhaps everyone is overtired, etc. The recess length is dependent on the circumstances. Did one party travel a long distance? Are there separate rooms in which each party can caucus or relax?
3. Introduce new information; try to change the scope or shape of the issue causing the hang-up. Perhaps its importance can be

altered by combining it with an issue that logically would have been introduced at a subsequent time.

4. Set aside the issue temporarily. Write it down so that both parties can agree on the description as being representative. Then, when the issue is resumed later there will not be a question about its content, scope, etc.. Be sure to put the written material in plain view. Agree that either party may reintroduce the issue when either feels it is timely. Proceed to another issue.

  The set-aside is a potent method for moving issues to more favorable slots on an agenda, even an informal one. It is resequencing the order in which the issues are discussed. The set-aside works especially well in three circumstances. The first is when an issue is out of sequence relative to other issues. This may be due to poor planning, assumption errors, etc. The second is when the feelings or emotions of one or both parties about an issue become intense enough to override legitimate discussion. This may be due to loss of self-control. The third is when not enough trust has been developed to discuss an issue having a particular level of sensitivity.

  One potential outcome in set-asides is that on returning to the issue, both parties may hold to their original positions. They are no better off than before. They are also no worse off. A stalemate may recur. Another potential outcome to the set-aside is that it may evolve into withdrawal of the issue. The initiative of the parties may be dampened.

  The set-aside is underutilized by most negotiators.

5. Change one or both parties. This should always be done through a joint agreement. Substituting different people removes the necessity of carrying forward unfavorable reactions between the original negotiator and opponent. These reactions may not be anyone's fault. They may simply be a bad reaction to one another, as happens through poor personal chemistry. The change also removes the effect of statements by the original parties that turned onerous.

The argument against changing parties in the negotiation rests on two premises. The first is that the suggestion for the change will be perceived as a sign of weakness by the opponent. That does not necessarily follow. But if it was the opponent's conclusion, it would be temporary only. When the new negotiator was not shown to be weak, the opponent would abandon that premise. The second premise is that the replacement might cause a loss of position. Nuances or allusions that make intent more clear are not easily communicated to the replacing individual. This risk must be assessed when judging whether replacement is a viable option.

6. Forgo negotiation and move to mediation or arbitration. Introducing a third party changes the process, since the influence of the original two parties is irrevocably reduced. Three parties represent a different type of exchange than is represented by negotiations. If avoiding a total breakdown is important and nothing else does it, then a third party is warranted. This should be a last step. Mediators and arbitrators can only be considered successful when each of the two sides is equally unhappy.

In general, the outcomes that are successful are achieved through effort, patience, and fairness. These must be balanced by negotiator competitiveness and stubborn commitment.

The next chapter examines the use of negotiating teams.

CHAPTER 3

Use of Teams

The Father and His Sons

A Father had a family of sons who were perpetually quarreling among themselves. When he failed to heal their disputes by his exhortations, he determined to give them a practical illustration of the evils of disunion; and for this purpose he one day told them to bring him a bundle of sticks. When they had done so, he placed the bundle into the hands of each of them in succession and ordered them to break it in pieces. They tried with all their strength, and were not able to do it. He next opened the bundle, took the sticks separately, one by one, and again put them into his sons' hands, upon which they broke them easily. He then addressed them in these words: "My sons, if you are of one mind, and unite to assist each other, you will be as this bundle, uninjured by all the attempts of your enemies; but if you are divided among yourselves, you will be broken as easily as these sticks."

Aesop's Fables

The Use of Teams

The use of teams to negotiate, versus doing it alone, is increasing. There are good reasons. First, negotiations are becoming more complex, partly due to growing regulation of the private sector. This adds to the difficulty of doing business. Second, as more knowledge is made available about every field, individuals become more specialized. It is increasingly tough for one person to have enough knowledge to conduct anything but simple negotiations. Third, teams provide witnesses to what was said. The team concept reduces second guessing from others who were not present at the negotiations. There are more people who know how, what, and why the agreements were reached.

Team Value

One-half the value in the team approach is its broader perspective when considering issues. Each person on the team is the sum of his experience, intelligence, physical drive, biases, etc. These factors comprise one's capacity base. By adding people together, a partial overlap in these bases occurs. However, the non-overlapping areas extend the capacity base of the team. Figure 3-1 depicts this phenomenon.

The other half of team value is that negotiation often involves at least three distinct roles: the talker, the recorder, and the director. It is difficult for one person to accomplish all three effectively. Two people can do them well. Three are ideal.

The *talker* presents positions on issues. He does the negotiating. One talker is generally all that is needed. The talker must be able to think relatively quickly. He simultaneously must arrange items by priority and relate these to his overall goals. The talker's abilities should include using clear terminology, constructing good examples, being sensitive to timing, and being understanding of others. Common sense and judgment are absolutely necessary for effectiveness as the talker. The style of presentation may range from "country" to "smooth." Style is of secondary importance. The talker is the most active of the three roles; it consumes the most energy. Stamina is an important asset for anyone filling this role.

The *recorder* must be a good judge of when a concession is made by his side or gotten from the opponent. He should instinctively know

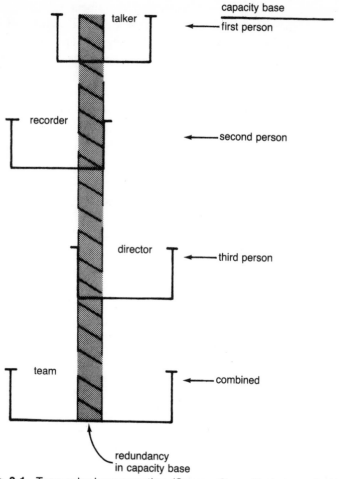

Figure 3-1. Team roles in perspective. (Source: *Group Techniques for Program Planning,* A.L. Delbecq, *et al.)*

what should be preserved in notes. He must be able to write things down while still listening to subsequent discussion. The recorder's abilities should include evaluating agreements clearly, writing concisely, and having excellent memory and recall. A human recorder is much better than a machine. Not all of the conversation that takes place needs to be retained.

For example, a sample of ten negotiations were totally recorded. Some were as brief as half a day, and one required a week. Only 6%-23% of the data (based on the number of total minutes) were judged critical. This estimate is supported by others who frequently negotiate. However, a caution is necessary about recording in any form. Later on, a legal dispute encompassing the negotiations might happen. Any record could be called as trial evidence. Retention of negotiation meeting records must be assessed against the risk of their being used in litigation. On balance, it is generally best to have well-kept and accurate notes. This should not be a problem in legitimate negotiations.

Example

An FTC price-discrimination hearing revolved around price breaks given by a supplier to large distributors. An executive of the supplier kept notes during negotiations with these distributors. He found to his chagrin that these notes became part of the hearing. It was awfully tough to recall events of a year ago—to explain precisely what his notes meant during the price negotiation.

The role of recorder is passive. Listening is the most critical asset for anyone filling this role. It is always worthwhile to have an extra pen and paper for the opponent who may not think to bring them. If the negotiator's side is going to make a record, the opponent's side should have the same option.

Example

A three-month negotiation dealing with rates and costs took place between the former US Department of HEW and a state Blue Cross/Blue Shield group. The government people did not take notes. The Blues did. At the conclusion of the negotiations, the Blues supplied the documentation for both sides. Objectivity was the goal of the Blues. However, whenever a point was indistinct or open to interpretation, one can conclude which way it was decided.

The *director* monitors the direction of the negotiation. He attempts to keep the talker on track and away from danger areas. A strong sense of anticipation and being well organized are necessary skills. Directors must have prearranged signals with talkers so that a recess or caucus can be initiated, as the director may need to review something (e.g., is the talker straying from the predetermined objectives inadvertantly or on purpose?).

Negotiating is best developed by watching others who are skillful; having subsidiary roles on teams is a starter.

Team Limits

If teams are such a great idea, why are they not used more often? Five constraints operate to slow the growth of team use.

1. Economic constraint (cost). It is more expensive to use two or three people rather than one.
2. Availability and choice constraints (time). It is often tough to get the team together for planning, etc. It is done at the expense of the member's regular duties.
3. Coordination restraint (interaction). It is difficult to get the team members to operate within defined roles. Tight discipline is necessary for smooth interaction.

     This third factor is particularly vexing for several reasons. The team's cohesiveness can be destroyed when one member agrees with the opponents without discussion among team members. Another problem crops up often. One member may provide the opponent with data at the wrong time. Keeping non-talker team members quiet is a major hurdle. Having more than one talker opens up tremendous opportunity for the opponents to drive a wedge through one's team or position. However, using the expertise of the non-talker members of the team may be necessary to detail or support a particular point. This is allowable when the team member with the expertise acts only as a presenter of specialized information. He must then reassume his passive role while the talker reasserts the verbal role.
4. Cooperation restraint (status). It is imprudent to ignore differences in organizational rank among team members, especially

if they interact in other situations. For instance, a higher rank-ing individual may not be well equipped to serve in the talker role. However, this individual may also be uncomfortable about his personal security. He may place a high importance on status to balance out his security concern. In this instance, it is pragmatic to assign him the talker role regardless of skill limitation. However, the opponent's perception about the talker's organizational rank should not be of concern. The opponent will get whatever message is there when he sees the team operate.

5. Parity-with-limits constraint (number). It is best not to outnum-ber the opponent. If the opponent consists of one person, he might be put off by the presence of a negotiator's team. More important, experience shows that the minority number in a negotiation is superior in its success to the majority number. If numbers are equal on each side, up to three members per team is best. If the negotiation team has three members and the opponent team arrives with two, it may be worthwhile to reduce the negotiator's team to two members.

Next best is to have less numerical strength than the other party. If the opponent's team has more than three, the negotia-tor should be unconcerned. People who bring in masses for their side are asking for trouble. They compound the con-straints already discussed, and add to them the problem of possibly becoming over confident due to numerical superiority alone. Typically, this overconfidence evaporates once the un-manageability of their larger group becomes apparent.

Figure 3-2 presents a four-factor rating for evaluating team effective-ness.
Guideline: Conduct in-group bargaining before the negotiation be-gins; work with the team members to get everyone on the same track, etc. It is absolutely necessary to get team cohesion and alignment in advance.

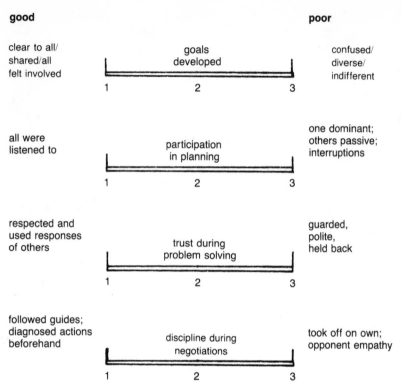

Figure 3-2. Evaluating team effectiveness. (Source: *Theories of Group Process*, G.L. Cooper.)

Guideline: Get protocol out of the way with the opponent at the start: who on your team has which role; establishment of ground rules; etc.

There are situations in which a team approach is ineffective. There are other situations where some of the negotiation should involve teams and where some should involve only the key team member. These are choices that must be made on an individual situation basis.

The next chapter discusses critical errors and how to avoid them.

CHAPTER 4

Three Critical Errors That Reduce Negotiator Effectiveness

The Stag at the Pool

A Stag overpowered by heat came to a spring to drink. Seeing his own shadow reflected in the water, he greatly admired the size and variety of his horns, but felt angry with himself for having such slender and weak feet. While he was thus contemplating himself, a Lion appeared at the pool and crouched to spring upon him. The Stag immediately took to flight, and exerting his utmost speed, as long as the plain was smooth and open, kept himself easily at a safe distance from the Lion. But entering a wood he became entangled by his horns, and the Lion quickly came up to him and caught him. When too late, he thus reproached himself: "Woe is me! How I have deceived myself! These feet which would have saved me I despised, and I gloried in these antlers which have proved my destruction."

What is most truly valuable is often underrated.
Aesop's Fables

Recurring Errors

There are many dos and don'ts regarding negotiating discussed throughout this book. However, there are three serious errors that have special importance because they occur often. They may well be inherent in the negotiating process.

1. Perspective error: concentrating on the present to the exclusion of the future.
2. Understanding error: ignoring built-in differences between oneself and the other party.
3. Utility error: misvaluing what one has to trade.

Perspective

Perspective errors indicate overreliance on short-term results. Actions are taken and proposals made during negotiations without concern for their future implications. The basic difference in attraction between the present and the future is easy to understand. Figure 4-1 presents reasons for this situation. Being less clear about the future should not lead a negotiator to build in problems that hinder or hurt agreement implementation.

Experienced negotiators attempt to balance current demands in agreements with potential future effects on implementation. They ask questions of their strategy: "What is the probable effect of this action on continuing relations with the opponent? Is the current situation linked in other ways to our organization, its image, or reputation? By contrast, people with the win/lose orientation concentrate only on the present. They view each negotiation, perhaps each issue, as a single instance. They seldom strike a balance between now and later.

The modifying factor on perspective is that there will only be one agreement with that party. This condition could affect strategy. However, it is very difficult to know for certain that the one agreement will not in some way find exposure to others who must be dealt with later. Therefore, even in single agreements, it is best to act as though there will be others with that party.

Understanding

Understanding errors happen when important differences between oneself and the opponent are not identified. This is excusable only for differences that are truly hidden. Subconscious differences are in that

Factors Influencing Concentration on the Present	Factors Contributing to Avoidance of the Future
Availability of a resource, often its scarcity.	Poorness of predictability, often related to unknown or uncontrollable actions changing what looked like a fixed course.
Immediacy of a need, often due to schedule or sequence demands.	Certainty of change. It is a given that change will occur.
Effect on the negotiator's performance, often related to job evaluation and output.	Impossibility of measuring just why certain past actions worked: how much was due to luck, how much to skill.
More knowns, often due to availability of data or access to similar past situations.	Possibility of extras (i.e. more contract clauses), often related to fear about change, increase, availability, etc.

Figure 4-1. Factors typically pushing attention in negotiations toward the present and away from the future. (Source: Sparks Consultants.)

category. Adequate planning before negotiations start provides a giant step toward removing or minimizing understanding errors. The time to pin point important differences is during preparation. These differences, if not dealt with, increase the degree of negotiating difficulty. Four of the more important differences and their possible clarifying actions are described here.

1. Unfamiliarity with customs of the industry. One should know how business is usually conducted in the opponent's arena. Likewise, one must communicate the "how" in his own arena.

Example

Oil companies generally pay supplier invoices in 90 days. That period can be cut if arrangements are made ahead of time. A contractor was doing engineering work for an oil-tool manufacturer. At completion, the contractor was not paid in the usual 30 days. Instead it was paid the way in which the manufacturer received its payments from oil companies. The contractor was deficient: It failed to identify the customary payment period in its customer's industry. The contractor incurred interest expense on the money it borrowed waiting for payment. Failures generate penalties.

2. Differences in value definitions. Where values are concerned, negotiators must recognize differences in definition and/or their basis.

Example

The definition of what is a fair business action can vary significantly between companies in different segments of the same industry. Primary metals producers enjoy larger dollar margins than do companies in the reprocessing or scrap business. Those in the scrap-metal business must therefore cut sharper deals to make a profit. Obviously, the definition of fair business action will be perceived differently by negotiators from these two industry segments.

3. Economic size differences. Negotiators must communicate their company's policy regarding economic differences due to company size. Smaller entities often feel that larger ones can better absorb certain costs. They may attempt to transfer these costs.

Example

A large utility had a policy of placing a portion of their orders with smaller businesses. An audit was made to determine the efficiency of the utility's purchasing department. The audit revealed that out-of-the-ordinary prepayments were made to a smaller supplier of specialized electrical controls. The supplier was asked to justify the size of the prepayments. It admitted that they were increased by three times the amount needed. The supplier felt the customer could afford to absorb the carrying charges better than it could. While no overcharge was involved, the time change in payments was in fact an economic change to the contract.

4. Unfamiliarity with local customs. One should always inquire about the pace of the business environment in which the opponent operates.

Example

A negotiator meets with an opponent located in Hattiesburg, Mississippi. He should expect to have a glass of iced tea, exchange pleasantries, etc. before getting down to the issues. This approach would not get far if attempted in the pressured business environment of New York City. Different industries have their own special pace. In general, banks and insurance companies seemingly crawl along compared to the frenzy at stock or commodity exchanges. But the bond traders in both banks and insurance companies are as rushed as any exchange trader.

Utility

Utility errors involve misestimating the worth of what one has to trade. Its importance to the opponent is incorrectly assessed, usually on the low side. The natural tendency is to undervalue what one already has, especially in excess. This is perhaps the most important of the three errors described. It can spell the difference in whether or not an equitable agreement is reached.

Example

Consider again the larger company trying to spread some business among smaller vendors to help their growth. Smaller vendors are usually less sophisticated. The margin of error tolerated for these smaller vendors may be higher than customarily permitted. The larger company is undervaluing its importance in helping smaller suppliers. It is not building within them the discipline needed to survive in more competitive situations. Likewise, the smaller supplier never appreciates real business tenets because it has become dependent on the largess of its benefactor.

Example

The technologically endowed West does not use its advanced expertise as a political weapon. Yet it is in competition with political systems pointed toward its eventual downfall. It fails to place a high enough value on the need for its technology by those competitors. Political concessions are not extracted for the benefit of the technology provided. The technology is often free.

The Negotiation Process: Summary

In this part, negotiation has been defined by identifying its characteristics. The advantages and limits of using teams have been discussed. Errors that typically crop up to impair reaching an agreement were described.

In this latter regard, negotiators must grasp the concept of utility. The value of anything depends largely on its actual or perceived utility to those who have it or want it. Quite often the value of X to someone is inversely proportional to the amount of X already held or controlled and proportional to the effort required to acquire X.

The next part of this book details the planning and preparation steps which help make negotiations successful and agreements workable.

Part II

Effective
Preparation

Effective Preparation: Introduction

The importance of preparation to effective negotiations cannot be overemphasized. The negotiator and opponent often have roughly the same amount of time available to prepare. They may not choose to use the time available for preparation. How each spends preparation time influences how the negotiation evolves and, probably, how it concludes. A brief review of win/lose versus win/win approaches illustrates the effect of emphasis during preparation on negotiations.

The win/lose proponents counsel spending time arranging the physical setting to convey a certain impression to others, placing seating to acquire a so-called power orientation for oneself, practicing body movements to convey non-verbal messages that will manipulate others, and similar activities. This preparation focuses on gimmicks. It is designed to gain an advantage over others representing different viewpoints. Other win/lose preparation involves selecting tactics outlined in Chapter 9. The shortcoming in win/lose preparation is not its questionable ethical base. Rather, it is its questionable assumption that the other party is easily intimidated. This approach assumes the other party will easily be manipulated by gimmicks. By contrast, the win/win proponent uses preparation time developing the merits of the issue. He uses systematic steps to ensure that his preparation is adequate. Win/win preparation offers the best chance for a balanced agreement. This is its value. When both parties feel they have gained, the agreement will more likely be carried through.

The actions examined in this part of the book are necessary regardless of the type of negotiation involved. The time spent on these steps is adjusted to the level of importance and to the complexity in any particular negotiation.

CHAPTER 5

Preparing for Negotiations

The Wild Boar and the Fox

A Wild Boar stood under a tree and rubbed his tusks against the trunk. A Fox passing by asked him why he thus sharpened his teeth when there was no danger threatening from either huntsman or hound. He replied "I do it advisedly; for it would never do to have to sharpen my weapons just at the time I ought to be using them."

Aesop's Fables

Skill, Not Art

Negotiation preparation is a skill, not an art. As such it is learnable. Beyond that, it is perfectable. Acceptance of this premise is the start toward becoming a more effective negotiator. By following the principles and methods suggested, the negotiator will discover how to sharpen his planning skills. To do this, he need not undergo a personality change. The need, instead, is to select the principles and methods which will work for oneself—those which will fine-tune one's planning technique and fit one's capabilities.

Estimating

In negotiations, both parties have information that is

1. Complete about the other party in some areas.
2. Incomplete about the other party in some areas.
3. Shared with the other party.

Where information is incomplete, one must make estimates. Negotiators who plan sufficiently, automatically improve the effectiveness of their estimating. Proper planning reduces the number of unknowns that must be considered. The range of chance occurrences that might upset the estimate is narrowed.

Preparation

Three actions comprise the main preparation for negotiations.

1. Collecting and organizing data.
2. Settling questions.
3. Reviewing data and aligning position.

Figure 5-1 shows the amount and relationship of preparation time usually devoted to each action. It includes adjusting attitude, an action that is discussed in the next chapter. Of course, before preparation starts, three overall questions should have been considered.

1. Should we do business with this party?
2. Is he trustworthy?
3. Is the timing right for these negotiations?

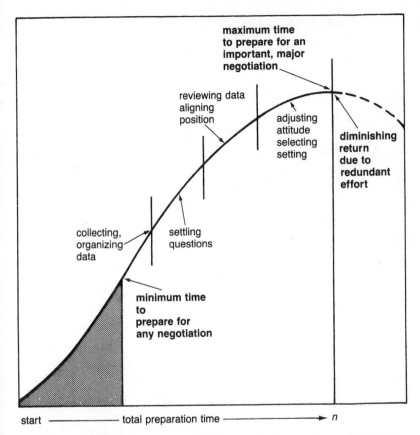

Figure 5-1. Comparison of amounts of time typically spent on each preparation action. (Source: Sparks Consultants.)

Collecting and Organizing Data

The process of getting data together and into usable form during preparation for negotiations can be divided into six steps:

1. Assembling facts and assumptions.
2. Dividing data into categories.
3. Establishing settlement ranges.

   4. Assigning bargaining methods.
   5. Selecting a starting place.
   6. Constructing a matrix.

By doing the first through fifth, a negotiator has a good chance of being ahead of his opponent. Many people are not disciplined enough to prepare correctly. By doing the sixth step, a negotiator almost ensures himself an advantage. Many people cannot conceptually handle this sixth step, even though it looks easy. All six steps require only a little time for a brief negotiation. They might require several days for an important issue. For complex negotiations, like those in mergers, acquisitions, or with unions, the steps might require several weeks or months to complete.

Facts and Assumptions

   The first step in preparation is assembling facts and separating them from assumptions. Facts are data that can be documented. They are non-disputable through support. They should be gathered in one folder or listed on one page. The letter F should be entered at the top of all fact data. This makes it easily identifiable later.

   Assumptions are information which must be drawn based on incomplete knowledge. Folders or pages of assumptions should each be marked with the letter A at their top. This keeps them from being mistaken for or mixed with factual data. Nothing is as weak in negotiations as assertions that are not backed by fact. If not tracked properly, assumptions might lead a negotiator to accept something as concrete that is actually clay. Some assumptions are always going to be necessary. The negotiator must judge how much assuming has to be done in preparation. Some things can be left to be developed in the actual negotiation. The best guide to follow is to make only first-level assumptions. These are connected loosely to facts.

Example

A negotiator assumes no change in the circumstances between an approaching negotiation and those of past negotiations. This session is with the same opponent as in the past. It is on the same type of issue. The negotiator might conclude that the opponent will repeat doing business on the same basis.

This conclusion is a first-level assumption. It is based mostly on information available to the negotiator: past actions of the opponent, what appears to be similar environmental forces as before, and the absence of indicated change in internal policy at the opponent organization. It is an assumption because changes that alter things might not show up until the negotiation takes place.

Second-level assumptions are those connected to other assumptions. They should be avoided.

Example

A negotiator assumes that the business with an opponent is locked-up before negotiation. For instance, the negotiator may feel that the opponent cannot walk away or deadlock; his position is too weak. This conclusion could lead a negotiator to make inappropriate demands.

That the opponent is locked-up is an example of a second-level assumption. It stems from the untested assessment of weakness of the opponent's position. That assessment is a first-level assumption, however. It is based on the negotiator's information, judgment, and perspective. Negotiators must continually be alert to, and recognize the danger inherent in, second-level assumptions.

Major and Minor Points

The second step in collecting and organizing data is to divide facts and assumptions into two categories. One applies to major points. The other applies to minor points—from the negotiator's perspective. When the organizational and factual support available to each point is seen, its value may change and, ultimately, its category. The longer points of lower importance are dealt with, the greater the chance they will acquire unwarranted status. Points of lower priority during internal negotiations can be dispatched quickly. Simply put enough high-paid people into the negotiation. Their time value will facilitate resolution or disposition of the lower importance points.

There are two reasons for making the division into major and minor points.

1. The negotiator must know ahead of time which points he can be easier about than other points. He makes this evaluation based on which points are more critical, what potential loss or cost might be incurred to his position, and how assertive he must be before becoming easier. In effect, this is a score-keeping mechanism for use in the actual negotiation. Any points that end up being assessed as noncritical—neither major nor minor—should be excluded. They can only serve as gimmicks thrown in to confuse discussion. They falsely complicate issues.

2. The points comprising the issue should be alphabetized. This prevents the opponent from being informed or tipped-off about the negotiator's major/minor distinction. For instance, an agenda might be exchanged with the opponent. The opponent might base his analysis on the negotiator's first discussion point. Naturally, an opponent would exert the greatest leverage against the negotiator's major points. He hopes to extract for his side the most concessions possible. Spotlighting one's major points gives an unnecessary advantage to the opponent.

There is an efficiency-based argument advanced against preparing with alphabetized lists. If one's major points are not settled up front, the possibility exists that the negotiating time is wasted. These points might later be found to cause deadlock. This argument gives more weight to efficiency than to effectiveness.

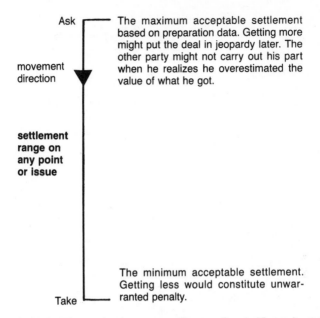

Figure 5-2. The Ask/Take settlement range. (Source: Sparks Consultants.)

Settlement Ranges

The third step is establishing settlement ranges for various points. These must be expressed in measurable terms, either by quantification or, as a second choice, through descriptive definition. Figure 5-2 depicts one set of these ranges—Ask/Take. When proposing a settlement, the negotiator would normally begin near his maximum, the Ask point. This is what he would like if it could be gotten. It must be realistic. For the opponent to accept the Ask level, he must be able to meet the obligation and complete his part of the agreement. If the opponent rejects the Ask level, the negotiator has room to move down the settlement range. He attempts to find a place satisfactory to

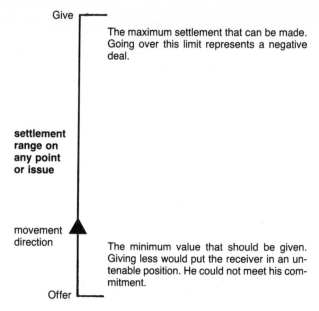

Figure 5-3. The Offer/Give settlement range. (Source: Sparks Consultants.)

the opponent. If the Take limit is reached and no settlement made, the negotiator has a clear stopping place.

When proposing a settlement, the negotiator might be making an Offer rather than presenting an Ask. Figure 5-3 depicts the other set of ranges—Offer/Give. The Offer is the minimum, the least-fair outlay. It is what the negotiator would like to part with if he could in exchange for what he wants. This must be reasonable. For the opponent to accept the Offer, he must be able to complete his part of the agreement and meet some of his needs. If rejected, the negotiator can advance up the settlement range to find a more satisfactory place. If the Give limit is reached without gaining a settlement, the negotiator again has a clear stopping place.

It is hard to fool oneself into accepting an improper settlement when the range is prepared correctly.

Example

A maintenance service contractor bid for a major overseas project at one-half the next lowest bidder. This contractor's bid was one-fourth lower than the internally developed estimate. The internal estimate showed the minimum needed by such a contractor to break even. The bid was accepted anyway. Half-way through the job, the contractor cratered. The customer ended up paying another contractor a premium to complete the maintenance service. The premium, when added to the original price paid the first contractor, was more than the next lowest original bidder. It was well above the breakeven figure originally developed internally by the customer.

In this example, the purchasing people should have shown the low bidder why they thought his bid was erroneous. They would have been better advised to get rebids. Alternatively, they could have covered the contract with a performance bond. This type of bond should be paid for by the contractor. Its cost should be added to the price charged the customer.

There is another factor supporting the need for pre-established settlement ranges. People often negotiate toward equity, at least in western cultures. Settlement ranges help establish equity. When equity cannot be established, expectations of one or both parties may be wildly out of touch with reality. Misimpressions then exist about what is possible, what is probable, and what is out of the question. This is a luxury a negotiator cannot afford. Nor can he assume his opponent wants to or is able to correctly establish equity. The negotiator must carefully develop realistic settlement ranges. However, modification can take place later during the work of "Reviewing Data and Aligning Position." Other changes can occur and be tracked during actual negotiation.

Settlements reached quickly are usually the result of a gap between the ranges of the negotiator and the opponent: for example, an Offer made that is more than an Ask of the other party, or an Ask made that is lower than the Offer of the other party. Poor preparation by one party is often the cause of the gap. Quick settlements may also result when both parties are well prepared. They clearly see the equity of an

Offer or Ask as it effects their own positions. If measurable limits cannot be set for a particular point, one of two things is the cause.

1. The point is, in reality, part of another point. It is in the wrong form, or has been misclassified. It should be reworked by incorporating it with the dominant point of the issue.
2. The point is not properly a part of the issue that will be negotiated. It should be dropped from the negotiator's list.

Bargaining Methods

The fourth step is to assign one of two bargaining methods to each point. The choice of method rests on the division made on the major and minor points and the measurement difficulty encountered in determining the settlement ranges.

The *trade-off* method is useful for lower priority points in an issue. In effect, the negotiator swaps one point to the opponent to acquire a different point from the opponent. The basis for trade-off bargaining is a preferential one as contrasted to investigative. Trade-off bargaining is caused by such things as time-limit dictates and point simplicity.

A caution is in order when considering trade-off bargaining. While the number of points or issues settled is high, equality of settlement is not necessarily part of the outcome. The more complex the issue, the more it is not a candidate for trade-off bargaining. Trade-off bargaining is especially useful for agenda setting at the beginning of actual negotiations.

The *problem-solving bargaining method* is useful for higher priority points or issues. In effect, the negotiator examines the merits of a point with the opponent from both their views. The attempt is made to arrive at a solution based on a combination of fact, respective merit, and the circumstances for each side. Problem solving is at the same time competitive and cooperative. A quality solution is the goal.

The output from problem-solving bargaining is lower than the output from trade-off bargaining; however, the quality of the settlement is often high. A caution is necessary when considering problem solving as a bargaining method. It should never be attempted unless there is adequate preparation. It almost always involves intricate moves by both parties in the negotiation. If these moves were unexplored by one party in planning, the settlement will probably be lopsided toward the other party. The steps for problem solving are described in Figure 5-4. Problem solving should generally be used for negotiation preparation involving teams.

The bargaining method available for a negotiator's use is not always at his option. It is sometimes predetermined as a result of

Sequence	Questions to Answer or Actions Required
Clarify the issue(s).	What is the tangible issue? Where do both parties stand: Do they see it the same way? Do they see it of equal importance?
Generate and evaluate possible solutions.	Each party identifies what it thinks are practical solutions. Each works with the other to evaluate those solutions.
Determine the optimum, not necessarily the ultimate, solution.	This involves settling on the solution most acceptable to both parties— one that has as much merit as possible, and one that might provide lasting results through the life span of the agreement.
Examine implementation.	Calculate how the solution will be carried out, identify potential problems, and include steps to deal with them in the agreement (if appropriate).

Figure 5-4. Problem-solving steps. (Source: *Clear Thinking,* R.W. Jepson.)

actions within his organization. This situation can impose severe limitations on the negotiator.

Example

The technical people in a multinational manufacturing company have the reputation for excessively working and reworking large project specifications. This is done during the project planning stage. They use most of the total get-ready time. This causes an habitual shortening of time for procurement needs. Procurement does not have time to accomplish all the steps for selecting suppliers stipulated in company policy. The result is often a trade-off bargain. The company pays a premium to get delivery of material within project completion schedule limits. Obviously, some vendors are able to determine that, at trade-off bargains, cost is secondary in importance to schedule compliance. Just as obviously, the technical people have more internal clout in this company than procurement people. These technical people repeatedly cause policy abortion, and there is no penalty to them for that action.

Starting Position

The fifth step is to pick one's starting position for the negotiation, in case it is needed. The position should be, headlined by a point that is likely common to both parties' agendas. This selection keeps the negotiator from divulging a point on his agenda that is not on the opponent's. The opponent does not gain the leverage he would if the negotiator exposed such a point. Alternatively, the possible starting point may be randomly chosen. The alphabetized list described under ''Major and Minor points can also be used. The opponent will have no clue to the negotiator's valuation of that point. No pattern is provided the opponent. He cannot develop strategy against a predictable approach by the negotiator. He must then work the issue. That is precisely where the negotiator has employed his preparation skill.

The Negotiation Matrix

The sixth step is determining relationships between various points by constructing a matrix. The matrix in this case is a rectangular array of points and resources. It makes resources common to two or more points readily identifiable. This step enables the negotiator to avoid a potentially serious problem. He might settle one point and later discover that the settlement boxed him in on a subsequent point. This sixth step can only be accomplished after concluding the other five. It is optional because sometimes it is unnecessary or impractical. If only one issue is being negotiated and its points have no common resource basis, a matrix would not be helpful. Most often the matrix is helpful. There is usually an important interrelationship of points and resources. Figure 5-5 illustrates a matrix for an issue.

Points		Resources	
		$	Delivery Time
Packing		10/doz	1 wk
loose, unwrapped		15/doz	1 wk
loose, wrapped		30/doz	3 wks
individually wrapped and boxed	range	10-30	1-3
Specification			
.006 tolerance		standard	n/c
.005 tolerance		+50/doz	n/c
.002 tolerance		+100/doz	1 wk
	range	0-100	0-1
Color			
regular paint		standard	n/c
special paint, any two colors		+2/doz	n/c
	range	0-2	ø

Figure 5-5. A sample negotiating matrix (Source: Sparks Consultants.)

Example

In the matrix in Figure 5-5, it can be seen that the three points—packing, specification, and color—all have price implications. They represent a related-by-resource set of points. Time implications exist for packing and specification, but not for color. Packing and specification become stronger related-by-resource points. As each point is discussed during negotiation, the negotiator may uncover data from the opponent that change his own position. He might then decide to revise his range, etc.

Example

If the total expenditure range available to the buyer in Figure 5-5 was $17 Give to $10 Offer, then the individual boxing option is automatically excluded. If loose wrapped is selected, the buyer can pay up to $15/doz and still get special paint at $2/doz. That puts the buyer at the Give limit. Unless specifications are special, the standard of .006 tolerance is acceptable. The buyer should determine if order size affects the packing cost. He might use a large order to reduce cost or get concessions on the paint, etc.

The negotiator uses a matrix to see the possible impact of individual settlements on the whole negotiation. He can choose to make a settlement tentative, based on the outcome of successive, related-by-resource points. He may opt instead not to highlight these point interrelationships. He would make all settlements tentative, based on final issue agreement.

Other Pluses From Matrix Use

Using a matrix has other values. First, it is the best way to demonstrate which variables are subject to control and which are not. This knowledge is critical because most negotiations involve variables. The variables are part of two kinds of problems.

1. Problems of competition: the need to select strategies without having full knowledge of the other side.

2. Problems of allocation: the need to assign available resources effectively to possible use or demand that exceeds the total resources available.

Second, most questions that confront negotiators involve making decisions under conflict conditions. The outcomes from these decisions are often less predictable. Therefore, the negotiator's intuitive ability and judgment play a key role. A matrix, while imperfect, aids in making judgment decisions. Third, the matrix is important because negotiations are not usually zero sum activities in which the outcome is totally one way or one sided. Fourth, negotiators can use matrix models when dealing with strategic questions. The models can

1. List payoffs from various strategies available to the negotiator and the opponent.
2. Highlight the strategies that offer the best chance of success for the negotiator.

Settling Questions

The second planning action involves answering four types of questions relating to the conduct of the negotiation.

1. Are there any possible penalties or alternatives?
2. How can weak points be strengthened?
3. What limits exist?
4. Who supports which issue?

Penalties and/or Alternatives

Questions regarding possible penalties relate to potential loss or a liability increase to the negotiator's side. For example, the cost of the negotiation ending in stalemate must be assessed. This helps determine how strong an effort should be made to avoid stalemate. The answer includes fixing the out-of-pocket preparation cost, looking at any alternatives for finding another party to negotiate with, achieving one's goals or maintaining one's operation and financial position if goals are not achieved, and estimating the effect on or risk to other relationships with the opponent, if any.

Example

A metals manufacturer purchases all the byproduct coke produced by several chemical plants. This type of coke is superior to other coke as a fuel source for the conversion of ore to ingots. It is sought after competitively. The chemical plants are a division of a company which has a joint venture in shipping with the metals company. When prices for the coke are negotiated with the chemical plants, they are conducted at arms length. Even so, the actions by negotiators for the metals company might ultimately affect the relationship involved in the shipping company joint venture. Actions contemplated by the metals-company negotiators should include an assessment of any probable impact on that other relationship. To do otherwise would be naive.

Seeing alternatives to any situation requires an ability to look beyond the obvious, to look past the usual answers one can identify easily. An exercise in finding alternatives illustrates how difficult it sometimes is to uncover them. The exercise is adapted from E. R. Emmet's *Learning to Think*.

Example

A table of eight numbers follows, and the task is to identify the ninth number(s) for the blank space in the table.

4	8	20
9	3	15
6	6	?

On investigation, one sees that there is no ratio across or down, i.e. no pattern. However, the numbers in the third column are all larger than the sum of the others in their own row. Pursuing this fact further, one can see that $4 + (2 \times 8) = 20$, and that $9 + (2 \times 3) = 15$. A rule can now be deduced for this table: by adding the number in the first column to twice the number in the second column, the sum is in the third column. Therefore, the number in blank space on the table should be 18: $6 + (2 \times 6)$. This would be a legitimate answer. However, does it cover the possibilities? Is there an alternative? The answer is yes. By looking down the numbers instead of across them, the third number in the two columns is the difference between the first and second number and the addition of one, i.e. $(9 - 4 = 5 + 1 = 6)$ and $(8 - 3 = 5 + 1 = 6)$. Now another rule can be deduced for this table: by adding one to the difference of the first two numbers of any column, the third number can be obtained. Therefore, the number in the blank space on the table should be 6 $(20 - 15 = 5 + 1 = 6)$. Is 18 preferable to 6 as an answer? There is no way to tell. Judgment then comes into play when selecting the best alternative. The negotiator must be able to identify the alternatives in order to apply his judgment to the fullest range of possibilities.

Strengthening Points

Another question that must be addressed concerns what options are available to strengthen a weak point. A primary option involves bluffing. It carries a two-part risk, however. The first part converts to a liability when a bluff is attempted and it fails. The loss incurred from a failed bluff is an increase in psychological advantage by the other party. This advantage may then persist through several subsequent points or issues. The second part becomes a negative because the exposed bluff creates a lessening of trust. The previous level of trust may be difficult to regain. This trust loss could cause negotiations to become protracted. One party seeks to establish thoroughly the other's real position in each new area to avoid being bluffed.

Even though the double risk is important, two circumstances make bluffing a potentially viable option. The first circumstance is when the negotiator has a weak case on what is to him a pivotal point. The second circumstance is when the stakes involved in gaining that point are high.

Example

In poker, it is foolhardy to try a bluff in a 5¢, 10¢, 25¢ three-raise-limit game. It is too easy for some player to stay in just to see the cards. However, in table stakes or pot limit poker, a bluff might work because the stakes make a wrong call expensive.

Guideline: In determining whether or not to plan a bluff, never do it unless absolutely necessary, and never tell anyone when it worked.

Limits

Determining the answer to the question of what limits exist gives the negotiator insight into boundaries confining his actions. These limits include the amount of actual authority the negotiator has or how far he can go on his own; how much additional spending he can commit; and how critical his say is if he decides to abort the negotiation. Other limits are the number of items that can be discussed in the negotiation, or how much time is available; points or issues that cause conflict with others if brought up at the same negotiating session; and schedule requirements of when the agreement is needed, which relates to lead time.

It is easier to find the limits arising from one's own situation than from the opponent's. Most opponent limits determined by the negotiator are the product of assumptions. The negotiator should confirm their validity as early as possible in the actual negotiations.

Support

Answering questions about who supports which issues gives the negotiator clues to their importance. It helps in drawing assumptions about the underlying cause of certain kinds of issues. The expectations of others may indicate the potential support available. Part of the how-much-support analysis can be made by looking at the design of the opponent organization. Figure 5-6 presents the usual locus of conflict as it relates to organization design. Apparent issues may not be the real objective of others.

Design of Opponent Organization	Area(s) of Primary Interest	Typical Conflict Points Due to Organization Design
Functional (manufacturing)	Size of own contributions to success versus other functions'.	Between functional areas. Does opponent represent dominant function or a subordinate one in his organization?
Product or service (technology based)	Growth of own area of business.	Between divisions. Is the opponent in a growing or shrinking division in his organization?
Process (metals, energy flow based)	Maintaining operational quality of own segment (technical excellence rules here).	Between segments. Is the opponent in a segment toward the front or more toward the end of the process cycle? (End people are often highly pointed to dependency and sometimes paranoiac.)
Matrix	Fluid	At all levels.

All designs may exist in one organization, but one design will predominate. The higher the opponent's job level, the broader his view and the less he suboptimizes. All the conflict points can exist in the same organization, but one will be more critical than the others.

Figure 5-6. Analyzing internal support available to opponent. (Source: Sparks Consultants.)

Example

A previously reliable supplier of bearings to a tool manufacturer began to miss critical delivery dates. No new element in the relationship could be identified by the customer as justifying the service drop-off. After erratic delivery repeated itself a few times, and the supplier could offer no assurance of correction, the tool company switched to another supplier.

Later that company discovered that its former supplier had committed almost all its output to a lucrative overseas contract. By having the tool manufacturer break-off the relationship, the supplier hoped to avoid an opportunistic reputation. It wanted to leave the door open if it needed that customer's business again.

Reviewing Data and Aligning Position

This third preparation action is a sequential set of four steps: review, brainstorming, testing, and "must" list development. During this part of preparation, an attempt is made to order the agenda. Issues or points are positioned so that they are in the best negotiating order. Usually this is from the more general to the more specific. This is not the alphabetical agenda the negotiator works from in actual negotiations. It is for his own perspective to assess the flow of issues or points within an issue.

Review

This first step is required; it is a review of the two previous actions: collecting and ordering data, and settling questions. The review focuses on information sufficiency and depth adequacy. Is the material too shallow? Is it unconvincing? The review often has positive results.

1. The support for one's position is improved by obtaining additional data. The value of this data makes the difference between a solid case versus only a good case.
2. Coordination between the negotiator and any back-up that might be required is tightened. This includes any technical presentations by experts who would not be a part of the continuing negotiation meetings.
3. Any final questions are cleared up and gaps in knowledge of any team members are filled.

4. The mix of information to be used is smoothed out. The more important parts are mixed with less important parts to aid in getting opponent receptivity. An opponent bored or dulled by lack of variety or texture might miss the convincing merits of the negotiator's side.

The methods for attaining a high level of opponent receptivity are discussed in Chapter 11. Figure 5-7 shows the sequence for data evaluation and disposition.

Brainstorming

The second step is brainstorming; it is optional. The purpose of this step is to find any creative aspects to the data. These might provide an added dimension to the negotiator's position. Its strength relative to the opponent's position might be increased.

In brainstorming:

1. A group of people sit in a room for a brief period, usually no more than an hour. They examine a well-defined point or issue.
2. Each person makes a statement about the subject. He is uninhibited by any rules, and can move in any direction. The statements require no amplification.
3. These statements are recorded without either a challenge to their validity or probing for more detail. In fact, there is no discussion at all.
4. The ideas are reviewed. Any that provide previously unthought of weight to one's position are retained.

Brainstorming does not always produce an improvement. Its chance for success is dependent on the acceptance of the premise that it usually uncovers creative aspects. There are well-run, successful companies that do not hold with the premise. Brainstorming works well in organizations that foster freer-flowing interchange between

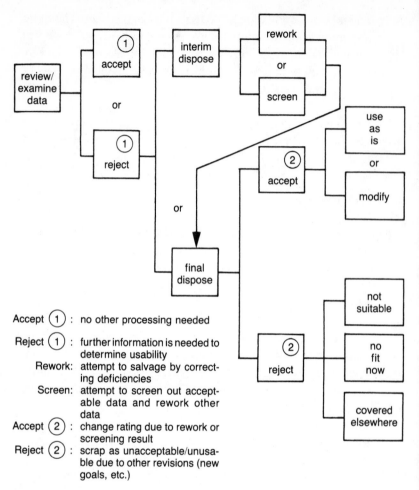

Accept ① :   no other processing needed

Reject ① :   further information is needed to determine usability

Rework: attempt to salvage by correcting deficiencies

Screen: attempt to screen out acceptable data and rework other data

Accept ② :   change rating due to rework or screening result

Reject ② :   scrap as unacceptable/unusable due to other revisions (new goals, etc.)

Figure 5-7. Data evaluation and disposition sequence. (Source: Sparks Consultants.)

authority levels as part of their normal operating style. Brainstorming can be a useful tool during negotiations for figuring out a way to break a stalemate.

Testing

The third step is to test out the strength of the position and to get it correctly aligned. This is arduous; it is also required. This is the opportunity to correct weaknesses and mistakes at minimal cost. The opponent corrects them for the negotiator at greater cost during the negotiation. Without this step the validity of the preceding preparation can only be determined during actual negotiation. That is a most unattractive alternative. A well-executed trial step reduces the potential for disaster to almost nil. Trial involves three tasks:

1. Someone takes the role of the opponent. This should be someone other than the negotiator. It should also be someone who has not been in the preparation effort. It helps if the individual serving as the opponent has been previously exposed to the opponent or his organization. It is very useful if he has been opposite the opponent in negotiations. This person should be supercritical. He should be someone not threatened in the opponent role—perhaps the negotiator's organizational superior.
2. The surrogate opponent gives the negotiator's position a working over whenever he perceives or finds a weakness in preparation of back-up data, or finds hesitancy about the facts.
3. On-the-spot adjustments are made and incorporated into the negotiator's position. Strategic moves are developed to increase chances for success.

Trial has two major shortcomings. It cannot duplicate the personal chemistry between the negotiator and his opponent. Nor will the surrogate opponent have all the current information available to the real opponent for evaluating various positions.

"Must" Lists

This fourth step is required. It consists of compiling a checklist of data that must be communicated to the opponent. These data are needed regardless of when a settlement is reached. Without such a list, an agreement could omit a critical item or a necessary routine item. The negotiator would then have to contact the opponent later and discuss the omitted item. The opponent's response might be unfavorable, such as:

1. Refusing to accept that item's inclusion in the agreement. A deal made is a deal to be kept.
2. Reopening the negotiation because the opponent had also inadvertently left out data. He can think of other items that should be discussed.
3. Raising the question of negotiator trustworthiness. Is this an attempt to slip by something extra?

The situation can occur where a "must" piece of data is inadvertently left out of an agreement. If it does, what is the best approach to the other party? The contact basis should be "Do you remember when we talked about . . ." rather than "I forgot to mention. . . ." The negotiator should be prepared to encounter a penalty charge in some form. The opponent will want a quid pro quo in order to get the "must" item included in an agreement.

Example

A company temporarily hired a technical specialist to help solve a particularly vexing problem in an overseas operation. Some of the work was to be done in the United States and some on-site. The fee and expenses were negotiated and agreed to; a contract was signed. The specialist later discovered that a tax on his earnings overseas would be due the foreign government. The company had not brought this point up in negotiating the fee. The specialist was not familiar with tax considerations in overseas work and therefore did not ask about them. The specialist was able to renegotiate his contract to include coverage of the overseas tax. But the question of trust had been raised. It created a distance between the specialist and the company people. Their relationship was cool and formal.

The "must" list is an underutilized tool in negotiations.

The next chapter describes how the negotiator can set his attitude to help launch the negotiation on a productive course.

CHAPTER 6

Attitude, Physical Setting, and Clock Time

The Two Bags

Every Man, according to an ancient legend, is born into the world with two bags suspended from his neck—a small bag in front full of his neighbor's faults, and a large bag behind filled with his own faults. Hence it is that men are quick to see the faults of others, and yet are often blind to their own failings.

Aesop's Fables

Adjusting Attitude

There are five steps that lead to establishing the attitude and mental set that foster successful negotiation.

1. Remove as many self-constructed barriers as possible. Clinging to biases elevates them to obstacles. This is unproductive. The negotiator is well advised to review his biases toward the opponent, even to write them on a note pad. This technique purges the biases temporarily. The negotiator can then work with the opponent without mixing in non-negotiating items. Along with any biases, it is worthwhile to jot down any feelings

that might impair negotiating progress. Afterward, the negotiator can reread his list and reinstall the biases in his mind.

Guideline: Strive for controlled neutrality toward the opponent during negotiation.

2. Avoid the possibility of having to choose between conflicting personal needs and organizational objectives. Develop a strong attachment to organizational goals while subordinating personal needs at the emotional level. Orientation away from himself and toward his organization provides the negotiator the self-motivation necessary for success. It prevents competition from developing between personal and organizational goals.

Guideline: By narrowing his normal emotional range while in contact with the opponent, the negotiator can concentrate on strategy. He stays issue oriented.

3. Create as little stress as possible. The friction caused by the forces of drive and restraint and the intensity accompanying conflict have already been described. These sum to a stressful situation. There is no need to create additional stress on the opponent purposely. In fact, that is counterproductive. For the negotiator to get his message across clearly, the opponent must be receptive. Openness and some relaxation aid receptivity. Stress, on the other hand, creates tension. Defensiveness and a lowering of receptivity follow. Stress also consumes energy that is better expended in gaining viable solutions to the conflict in the negotiation. If the opponent's energy is depleted by stress, he might hole-up. The negotiation then becomes protracted unnecessarily.

Guideline: Do not contribute to stresses already present. Of course, the negotiator cannot be responsible for strains that the opponent concocts on his own.

4. Gain as much understanding of the opponent's values as possible. Prior to negotiations, whenever practical, the negotiator

should spend some time with the opponent. This time represents an opportunity for developing a relationship that facilitates an agreement. The negotiator can use it to reduce barriers by establishing his objectivity. He can convey his respect for the opponent's position. The negotiator should look for similarities between himself and the opponent. These should be highlighted. They might enhance the working relationship of the two parties. The negotiator can convey his own thoughts to help set a professional level and tone for negotiating conduct. He can identify areas of difference unrelated to the negotiation. These should be skirted to avoid ticking-off the opponent needlessly.

Guideline: Be alert to what the opponent says in the time before the negotiation starts. Interpret those pieces of information that help provide a key to the opponent's personality. When most people outline things they are involved in, they generally show themselves in the best light possible. They also invariably include trivial particulars about things that mean a great deal to themselves. These slip out unconsciously. They describe a person's real passions.

5. Develop as great an understanding as possible of personal limits. The negotiator should review his personal habits, quirks, etc. He must become aware of anything that might interfere with his ability to negotiate. Broadly speaking, three categories are covered in this awareness: mental, physical, and emotional. An example of a mental habit that is harmful in negotiating is wandering attention. The negotiator's inability to concentrate might cause him to miss a critical concession. A physical constitution that works against effective performance is the inability to drink alcoholic beverages in one evening and think clearly the next day. Mental and physical limits are usually manageable if the time is taken to make them so. For instance, wandering attention can be corrected for the actual negotiating period. One can consciously direct attention to the subject under discussion. A person can discipline himself to defer alcoholic intake beyond his capacity before negotiating. It is the emotional category that is the problem. Very few

people can purge private serious concerns, e.g., a loved one seriously ill, being in a tough financial crunch, etc. However, negotiators must be able to leave their losses from a previous negotiation outside of a current one. Carrying one's losses forward to the next point, issue, or negotiation is a sure way to perform less effectively. It may even help the opponent to an easy victory.

Guideline: Know your own mental, physical, and emotional shortcomings. Shore them up whenever they might lessen negotiating effectiveness.

In brief, negotiators must distinguish between two types of involvement—personal and emotional. Personal involvement is necessary for self-motivation. Emotional involvement is a hindrance. It opens the way for impulse control to emerge. It is difficult to keep a disciplined approach under impulse control.

A Few Words About Message Sources

There are seven sources of messages received by one person from another. These sources are divided into two classes: auditory and visual.

Auditory Messages

Auditory messages have three sources:

1. Sound of voice.
2. Actual words used.
3. How rapidly the words are spoken.

All three auditory sources are valuable during negotiations for ascertaining a message's meaning. They are also valuable in identifying how strongly or moderately the sender feels about the message's subject. Techniques for using and receiving auditory messages effectively are discussed in Chapter 11.

Visual Messages

Visual messages have four sources:

1. The eyes and facial expression.
2. Tilt of the head.
3. Total body posture.
4. Movements of the body.

Of these, only the eyes and facial expressions have been scientifically documented. There is ample psychiatric and clinical psychological data on the meaning of eye movements and facial expressions. The problem confronting most negotiators in using these data is finding time to learn the multiplicity and meaning of facial-expression combinations and eye movements. Even if these were learned, a person can mask or control them through training.

The other three visual message sources can be grouped into mostly unresearched and unproven, but popular, "body language." The problem about these sources is the ease with which they can be controlled. The message sources of tilt of the head, total body posture, and movements of the body are readily manageable. It follows that they are less reliable as measures of an individual's real intent or message meaning.

Guideline: Negotiators should pay attention to all three auditory message sources and to eye movements of opponents during negotiations. They should process observed data from other visual messages in the same way they process those data in social situations, i.e. without particular special attention.

Guideline: When negotiating with people from different cultures, negotiators should first become acquainted with any particular physical constraints or movements that might be peculiar to those cultures, or at least different from their own culture.

A Few Words About Physical Setting

The question of what is a good site for the negotiation has been overblown. Anthropologists are split about the value of the physical site as to who comes to whom. Some say going to the opponent's location is a subliminal attack: the negotiator has invaded the opponent's territory. Other anthropologists claim it is a surrender to enter the opponent's territory. The fact is, if one is properly prepared, it makes little difference where the negotiation is held. The only exception is where some physical limit dictates the location. This could be the location of a volume of data or a need for site inspection. Negotiators should not be influenced by the location. They should realize that having the opponent select the site might remove some stress for the opponent. He will be more comfortable, and probably more receptive.

Example

The negotiator responsible for multimillion-dollar acquisition deals of a large hotel chain designed his office as the best place to negotiate. He has a generous conversational area, a smaller close area, and a formal area for rejecting points. This man has an excellent track record. Perhaps for him the office setting is important. However, his industry opponents almost always command smaller resources than he has. They almost always visit him at their own instigation. When going after financing from major banks and insurance companies, this same man has no hang-up about visiting their locations. He is equally successful at obtaining the financing his organization needs.

A Few Words About Clock Time

Each person has an energy cycle. At the high part of this cycle they are generally more alert. They are apt to perform at their best. The negotiator should try to schedule negotiations to correspond to the high part of his energy cycle.

Fifteen hundred negotiators attending Sparks' Negotiating Skills Improvement seminars were surveyed as to their energy cycle. The majority responded that their cycle was higher in the morning. Figure 6-1 shows this data.

The negotiator should keep his energy cycle in mind when traveling across time zones. For short periods of travel, he should arrange negotiating meetings to correspond to his customary time zone. The question of jet lag must be dealt with by some negotiators, but not all. Some are able to pump-prime their energies. They show no noticeable effect from across-time-zone travel.

Negotiators should watch the clock at each negotiation session. If no discernible progress is made within the first few hours, experience shows that little will be achieved. Under that circumstance, the guide to follow is to recess or reschedule that particular session.

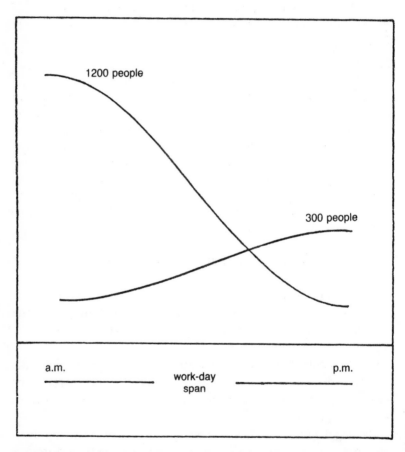

Figure 6-1. High/low energy curves for 1500 people who negotiate often (based on their own estimates). (Source: Sparks Consultants.)

Effective Preparation: Summary

In the final analysis, thorough preparation is as important as expertise to successful negotiating. Correct preparation ensures the negotiator that his case is the strongest possible. The negotiator hopes to gain the objectives that benefit his organization. He must, however, give some attention to the long-term-relationship effects of his actions and to possible alternatives if the negotiation fails.

Before the negotiation concludes, the negotiator should have thought out the impression he wants to leave with the opponent. Why give to chance what can possibly become a strategic benefit impacting future relations with the opponent? The last impression should be planned just as the other actions are planned. It is often what is remembered most at the parties' next encounter.

The next part of this book examines actual negotiations with the opponent. It delves into what works well and what to avoid.

Part III

Negotiations Conduct

Negotiations Conduct: Introduction

Less time is required to actually conduct a negotiation than to prepare adequately. The degree of success achieved during negotiation is influenced heavily by five actions of the negotiator:

1. Correctly categorizing conflict.
2. Possessing adequate self-protection.
3. Identifying opponent need orientation.
4. Managing power factors.
5. Gaining a high receptivity level.

These actions are treated individually in Chapters 7 through 11.

CHAPTER 7

Conflict

The Laborer and the Snake

A Snake, having made his hole close to the porch of a cottage, inflicted a mortal bite on the Cottager's infant son. Grieving over his loss, the Father resolved to kill the Snake. The next day, when it came out of its hole for food, he took up his axe, but by swinging too hastily, missed its head and cut off only the end of its tail. After some time the Cottager, afraid that the Snake would bite him also, endeavored to make peace, and placed some bread and salt in the hole. The Snake, slightly hissing, said: "There can henceforth be no peace between us; for whenever I see you I shall remember the loss of my tail, and whenever you see me you will be thinking of the death of your son."

No one truly forgets injuries in the presence of him who caused the injury.
Aesop's Fables

Correctly Categorizing Conflict

During negotiations conflicts arise; some are predictable, some not. The negotiator needs a model for comparing different conflicts. Figure 7-1 depicts a mental model of conflict that is useful. Its design originates from psychological research relating to the management of

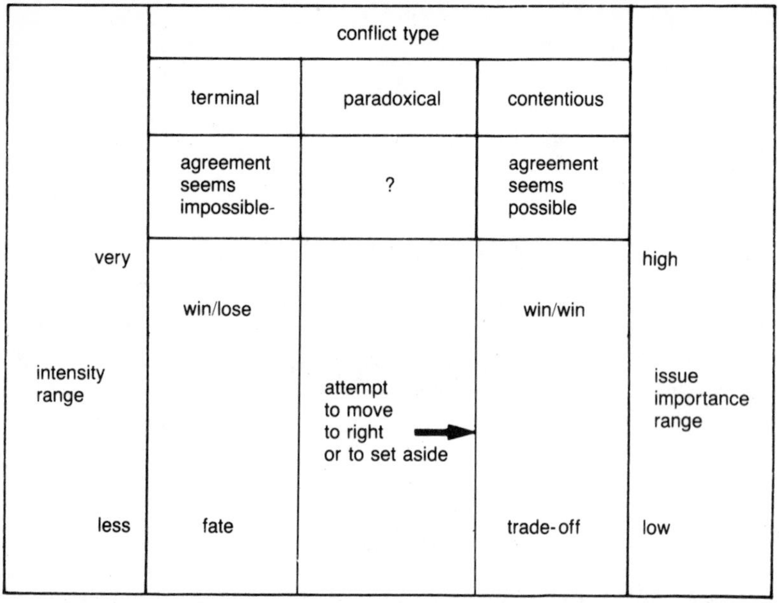

	conflict type			
	terminal	paradoxical	contentious	
	agreement seems impossible-	?	agreement seems possible	
very				high
	win/lose		win/win	
intensity range		attempt to move to right ➡ or to set aside		issue importance range
less	fate		trade-off	low

A negotiator adopting contentious position for a highly important point, finding no progress, eventually moves to terminal conflict. Otherwise he risks stalemate or deadlock.

Figure 7-1. A mental model of conflict by type and intensity. (Source: *Put Offs and Come Ons,* A.H. Chapman.)

group interactions. With this model the negotiator can make two key decisions regarding any given conflict. The first decision is to classify the conflict based on its solvability:

1. Terminal conflict appears to be impossible to solve by agreement. It is characteristically win/lose.
2. Paradoxical conflict appears to be unclear, its solvability questionable. It is often later found to relate to a point that was out of sequence; insufficiently defined; or in reality part of another

point, and best not examined separately. It is characteristically neither win/lose nor win/win.
3. Contentious conflict appears to be solvable. It is characteristically win/win.

The second decision is to classify the conflict based on its intensity:
1. Very intense conflict exists when the stakes involved are highly important to the negotiator and his opponent. They will be energetic and active in this situation.
2. Less intense conflict exists when the stakes involved are of minor importance to the negotiator and his opponent. They will be moderately energetic or passive in this situation. An offshoot of this level occurs when only one party does not care strongly about the issue being negotiated.

Negotiators exercising proper discipline do not react to a conflict until they have made both decisions. Otherwise, they increase the risk of acting incompatibly with either the solvability or intensity of the conflict.

Examples

Finding oneself incontrovertibly locked in a win/lose struggle over a point of minor importance is a failure to classify intensity.

Becoming mired in a debate which offers no possibility of any useful outcome is a failure to classify solvability.

These examples do not apply to union negotiations. In union negotiations intense conflicts are often artificially created over inconsequential points as a diversionary tactic, to wear down the other party, or to delay settlement until the "proper" amount of time has elapsed. In general, union negotiations lack the reality available in other negotiations. Union negotiations often reflect a set scenario that must take place regardless of the actual amount of conflict between the parties.

Actions and Outcomes by Conflict Type/Intensity

Terminal Conflict

Terminal conflict involving a highly important point generates win/lose actions by one or both parties.

1. Embracing one's own position as praiseworthy. This becomes especially critical when one believes his own position is the only real position possible. Simultaneously with downgrading the other party's position, one's judgment becomes distorted. Objectivity is lost.
2. Attacking or counterattacking the other party by belittling his position and casting doubt on its validity. This is followed by demonstrating its inferiority to one's own position. Conflict aggravation increases. Suspicion and subjectivity are promoted.
3. Developing a negative stereotype of the other party. This further provokes him. Respect and confidence in the other party erode.

Terminal conflict distorts one's ability to think clearly about and understand the conflict. It is difficult to keep perspective. Actions become incomprehensible as the win motive overwhelms logic and reason. The commonalities in the two positions of the parties are minimized. Their differences are highlighted.

The outcome of a win/lose battle is predictable. One party is the victor, one the defeated. Both are marred. The chance is reduced that subsequent issues will be handled in a mutually beneficial way. Any agreements reached will probably not be genuinely supported by both parties. A win/lose battle has three results:

1. Competitive feelings and mutually disparaging attitudes become ingrained.
2. Perception that either parties' offerings are well intended is blocked.
3. Antagonism, hostility, and distrust are produced and reinforced.

The terminal conflict over a point of minor importance involves actions relying on fate by one or both parties.

1. Avoidance: the use of any chance mechanism, such as coin-tossing, to select a decision. Fighting it out is avoided. Yet reaching a settlement some way other than chance might be seen as a loss of face.
2. Delay: the use of any continuance mechanism, such as "not now, but later," to defer a decision. The point or issue is rescheduled or put into limbo.

The outcome of fate is that bloodletting is avoided. However, the decision reached is seldom based on the relative merits of the issue. When more facts become known, fate may not turn out to be a better choice than other methods. Its use can produce additional and even greater difficulties than were originally encountered.

Paradoxical Conflict

The paradoxical conflict is best handled by the set-aside method described in Chapter 2. This allows the parties to proceed to other issues. They temporarily isolate an issue through neutrality. The set-aside permits both parties to retain their independence and definitions until later. They may even conclude that mutual indifference is ultimately best for the issue.

Contentious Conflict

Contentious conflict involving a highly important point or issue promotes win/win actions by one or both parties:

1. Feeling optimistic toward oneself and the other party. Understanding and respect for the other party's position emerge; a collaborative climate results. However, strong competitive drives are not reduced.
2. Clarifying the issue through definition. Issue resolution based on the merits of each party's position is emphasized. Accommodation is avoided.
3. Exploring what the facts are and agreeing up on these. A range of possible settlements is developed. The either-one-answer-or-deadlock approach is avoided.
4. Agreement being reached by both parties contesting each other's positions. While acceptable to both parties, the agreement is probably not of equal value to both. It is practical.

The outcome of a win/win collaboration is predictable. Both sides achieve at least some of their objectives. A win/win collaboration has three results:

1. Commitment to a genuinely sound agreement attained through mutual effort.
2. Establishment of a base for working together in the future.
3. Reenforcement of trust by the parties in one another.

The contentious conflict of less intensity involves trade-off actions by one or both parties.

1. *Swap:* splitting the difference between the positions. Both parties consciously adjust their positions to avoid a stalemate.

Another form of swap is intentionally exchanging one point for another.

2. *Deprivation:* giving up part of one's resource roughly equal to the resource amount yielded by the other party in reaching an agreement. A partial loss is preferable in some cases. Non-agreement may mean a total loss. Deprivation can also occur when the parties recognize that continued debate is more costly than settlement. Previously unacceptable modifications to both parties' positions are accepted.

The outcome of a trade-off is an acceptable agreement, but not necessarily the better agreement. The tension that existed is relieved, but the harmony maintained may only be on the surface. One or both parties may be left uncommitted or dissatisfied.

The next chapter discusses protection from intimidation.

CHAPTER 8

Intimidation and Protection

The Fawn and His Mother

A young Fawn once said to his Mother, "You are larger than a dog, and swifter, and more used to running, and you have your horns as a defense; why, then O Mother! do the hounds frighten you so?" She smiled and said: "I know full well my son, that all you say is true. I have the advantages you mention, but when I hear even the bark of a single dog I feel ready to faint, and fly away as fast as I can."

No arguments will give courage to the coward.
Aesop's Fables

Bolstering Resolve

Any negotiator can be intimidated, given the right set of circumstances. The source of the intimidation may be the opponent, a situation, or, as it often is, within oneself. It makes sense to take steps that will reduce the chance of being intimidated from either external forces or internal forces. There are two steps which aid in bolstering resolve. They retard being overawed or cowed.

First, *develop a positive self-image* as a negotiator. Self-image is one's concept of his specific role in a given situation. It is the conscious part of personality derived from contacts with reality. It largely directs one's self-esteem, e.g., what is thought by oneself about oneself. A positive self-image enables the negotiator to withstand the pressures inherent in the negotiating process, balance selective risks against possible losses, view change with perspective, and stay on course. The nervous person, the worrier, is unable to maintain a positive self-image.

Along with maintaining a positive self-image, a negotiator needs to be highly committed to his goals. Emphasizing the rightness of sticking with a valued belief or idea helps achieve commitment. By merging his own interest with his organization's negotiating goals, the negotiator is difficult to dislodge through intimidation. The merger doesn't require emotional involvement. It does require personal involvement. Personal involvement is a necessary cornerstone for a high level of motivation.

Second, the negotiator should *enact external governances* that set up protective limits to negotiating actions. These are policies or guidelines. They typically require higher authority approval before certain changes in position can be made by the negotiator. Examples of the changes often covered by protective limits are the acceptance of other than present objectives, and going outside the usual terms and conditions.

Developing a positive self-image is the more useful of these two steps. Fears are often self-induced. They can have their roots in emotional conflict. They are sometimes self-fulfilling. As Job said, "Hardly have I entertained a fear that it comes to pass and all the evils I foresee descend on my head."

Private- Versus Public-Sector Protective Limits

The tightness of external governance on a negotiator is markedly different between the private and public sectors, although similar in design. External governance in the private sector is more amenable to change; it is organizational-policy based. The authority to change that policy is readily identifiable. In the private sector, policies generally have the objective of supporting what is to be produced by the organization. They are therefore function oriented.

Example

A machine-tool company had a purchasing policy forbidding progress payments. Purchasing people violated that policy, with tacit executive support, whenever that action contributed to getting the cost of a purchased component reduced. These progress payments were always calculated on a per cent completion of order; never by date. In effect they reduced the interest cost of the vendor. He passed that saving on to the company.

In the public sector, external governance is tied to administrative procedure. This is based on interpretation of legal constraints and requirements. The authority to authorize or make changes is often far removed from those who are enacting the charter. In the public sector, policies generally have the objective of supporting how something is done. They are therefore process oriented. Prohibitive external governance, while acting to retard intimidation, also acts to inhibit the evolution of creative solutions. These are the very solutions through which both parties gain more than was originally thought possible.

Guideline: When negotiating with regulatory agencies and other governmental bodies, first identify which forces dominate the agency. For instance: Is it a consumer group? Is it the industry that is being regulated? With the perspective of which constituency is being served, the decision process of the agency can be tracked. Strategies can be selected that are appropriate to influencing that decision process.

Understanding Commercial Contracts

The use of commercial contracts is increasing in all types of business negotiations. Commercial contracts can be intimidating, especially when one is not trained in legal matters. Negotiators must understand the basic elements of commercial contracts. They can then identify when to seek and utilize experts with legal training. The basic elements of commercial contracts can be grouped into terms and coverage.

Terms

1. A contract is a written document embodying a particular transaction, agreement, etc.
2. A buyer is the purchaser or user.
3. A seller is the vendor or supplier.
4. A provision is a substantive matter; provisions are sometimes called "terms."
5. A breach is an obligation that has not been carried out due to the fault of either or both parties.
6. A stipulation describes the product or service that is to be provided by a vendor and the price which is to be paid by the buyer.
7. A contingency is a happening that might arise during performance of the contract owing to foreseeable or unforeseeable changes in circumstances.
8. A master form contains all elements of a transaction in a single document detailing the vendor's total responsibility in regard to a particular situation.
9. Separately enforceable documents divide various contract elements into phases of the transaction.
10. A master form with amendments reflects changes to the master form decided during negotiations; it must not predate the master agreement.
11. A force majeure is an event that relieves all parties of responsibility for carrying out the agreement. These events should be spelled out.

12. A zipper clause states that all agreements are in the agreement and no other elaborations are needed.
13. A most-favored-nations clause obligates the parties to pass on benefits to one another that are no less favorable than those given to others.

Coverage

Commercial contracts should include, in addition to the previously stated terms, clauses that cover several important points.

1. Amendments should be in writing. (Negotiators should avoid spoken agreements or modifications to written agreements.)
2. Warranties should be clear. (Implied or expressed warranties should be described in the same terms.)
3. Assignments of rights under the contract should be limited or forbidden. (Nonassignability without written permission is the rule and, then, the assigning party should not be relieved of its responsibilities.)
4. Authority of signers to obligate their organizations should be spelled out.
5. Seller's business should be covered. (But if seller or buyer goes into bankruptcy, the agreement of both parties is terminated.)
6. Compliance with federal regulations should be required. (Statement should be included that holds the buyer harmless if the seller fails to comply with applicable laws.)
7. Confidentiality and non-disclosure of material and information should be protected from third parties. (This includes both written and unwritten data.)
8. Indemnification in general should be stipulated. (To ensure the correct language, a legal opinion is required.)
9. Limitation of liability should be stated in dollars, percent, or other specific determinant.

10. Notices should be described by the method in which they are to be transmitted. (This should include designation of who is to receive them and in what format.)
11. Survival beyond completion of the contract should include those contract parts as necessary, such as confidentiality. (Each contract part should be referenced for specific provisions that survive contract completion.)
12. Waivers where any party relinquishes its enforcement right of a specific contract part should be stated to not void, waive, or modify any other terms or conditions or to relinquish subsequent performance on such items.
13. Patent, trademark, and corporate indemnity should be provided by seller. (This should include all expenses that might be sustained, whether or not an infringement claim against the seller is successful.)

Negotiators should remember that substance of a commercial contract is the primary concern rather than the forms used. Compliance with the Uniform Commercial Code is important. A legal review of any commercial contract can ensure this compliance.

The use of legal experts in commercial contract evaluation must be differentiated from their general use as advisors. Negotiators should answer the question "Do I need the legal expert for his knowledge in a given area, or do I want him as a general advisor?"

Guideline: It is often best to use experts, legal and otherwise, mainly for their specialized knowledge. For other negotiating needs, such as strategic decisions, it is best to rely on common sense, the objective being sought, and the negotiator's past experience.

Guideline: Whether or not a commercial contract is involved, the negotiator should check on the past performance or record of the other party: Do he and his organization deliver as advertised? Do he and his organization live up to agreements?

Evaluating Visuals

Visual data such as charts, graphs, and pictures indicate a level of objectivity that may be intimidating. Negotiators should examine visual data provided by opponents to ensure that it is not quasi-quantitative. Most visual data contain only a sample of the total data they are supposed to represent. All samples have built-in biases. To uncover these biases, the negotiator should use five checks.

1. Always check pictures. To make a greater impact, pictures are often out of proportion to the difference they are used to represent.

Example

☐ X has grown by twice as much. ☐ But the picture shows X at four times, rather than twice as much as its former self.

2. Always check charts and graphs to ensure they use the same units up and down as are used sideways.

Example

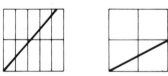

The diagonal line in the first drawing is twice as steep as in the second because the vertical lines are closer together than the horizontal lines.

3. Always check completeness. By cutting out the middle of a chart, it visually looks as though the differences between compared items are greater than actual.

Example

Without knowing the total column height, the importance of the difference between the columns cannot be seen.

4. Always check the term "average." Is it the arithmetic average, or is it the median (mid point) or the mode (most frequently occurring)? The median usually tells most about a situation.
5. Always check to be sure tables and charts have scales where needed.

Guideline: Ask the four critical questions about visual data:

1. Is the source genuine?
2. Is the sample large enough to be reliable?
3. Are raw figures used or have percentages been substituted? If the latter, do they alter the emphasis of the data?
4. Does it make sense?

The next chapter describes opponent need orientation.

CHAPTER 9

Opponent Needs

The Peasant and the Apple Tree

A Peasant had in his garden an Apple Tree which bore no fruit but only served as a harbor for the sparrows and grasshoppers. He resolved to cut it down, and taking his axe in his hand, made a bold stroke at its roots. The grasshoppers and sparrows entreated him not to cut down the tree that sheltered them, but to spare it, and they would sing to him and lighten his labors. He paid no attention to their requests, but hit the tree a second and third blow with his axe. When he reached the hollow of the tree, he found a hive full of honey. Having tasted the honeycomb, he threw down his axe, and looking on the tree as sacred, took great care of it.

Self-interest alone moves some men.
Aesop's Fables

Need Theory

Current need theory is based on the research done by Abraham Maslow. He closely observed disturbed people because they exhibit distinct behavior unencumbered by societal constraints. His conclusions were converted to a general behavioral theory. One conclusion useful to negotiators is that opponent needs often influence style and actions as well as receptivity to the negotiator's position. In general, people have needs in all the areas described in this chapter. Some are dominant at one time, others at another time. It is neither simple nor easy to uncover and identify correctly the need orientation of someone else. Negotiators who want to be more successful must develop the skills needed to make the correct needs analysis.

Identifying Opponent Need Orientation

Finding the opponent's dominant need orientation enables the negotiator to work better with him. The first opportunity for the negotiator to identify opponent need orientation is before negotiation starts. Second, he should be alert for keys to opponent need orientation during the negotiation. There are four basic need orientations for opponents.

1. *Low risk:* an overriding concern with protection against threat or danger to one's position, or for the safety of one's objectives. A negotiator identifying low risk as a dominant need for the opponent should emphasize the certainty aspects of his position. These lower the risk in a potential agreement. Negotiators do not need to artificially create, suggest, or imply what is not there. Almost any position has some elements of certainty. The negotiator simply spends more time on these. He devotes less time to other aspects of his proposed solution. He attempts to describe things in terms with which the opponent can live.

2. *Association:* preoccupation with engaging in social interaction with others, including the negotiator. Acceptance by others is crucial to this opponent. The negotiator must make it absolutely clear that the opponent is well regarded and accepted. Emphasizing areas of commonality in the two positions is important. This conveys feelings of belonging, sharing, and, ultimately, mutual acceptability to the opponent. The negotiator should also emphasize areas personally shared with this

opponent, such as similar job specialities, interests, ideas, and experiences. The relationship is reenforced. The negotiator should steer clear of commenting on areas where the opponent expresses negative feelings and opinions. Agreeing with an opponent that certain things are awful requires using a negative expression pattern. The results of this pattern are described in Chapter 11. It is not desirable.

3. *Recognition:* the strong drive for personal status. Opponents having a strong recognition need are concerned that they be perceived correctly by others. They want to be seen in the same vein as they see themselves. The negotiator must dwell heavily on those aspects of his position that benefit the stature of the opponent or even his organization, if that is where the opponent's interest lies. Identifying a gain for both the opponent and his organization gives the negotiator the best chance for a favorable reaction. Status is important to an opponent with this need orientation. The negotiator whose title conveys a lower organizational status than the opponent's may find tough sledding.

4. *Achievement:* accomplishing tasks in a context that permits the action to serve itself. This opponent is at the other end of the spectrum from one who is low risk. The creative and breaking-new-ground aspects of the negotiator's position should be highlighted.

Maslow denoted a basic need level below low risk. It involves concern for food and shelter. This need is unlikely to be encountered in a negotiation. An opponent with such a fundamental need orientation would be in too weak a position. He could not offer much resistance. The lower level the need orientation, the less complex it is. Figure 9-1 depicts this fact. Theoretically, it should be less difficult to influence opponents oriented to low risk than those with an association orientation. In actuality, complexity as it relates to

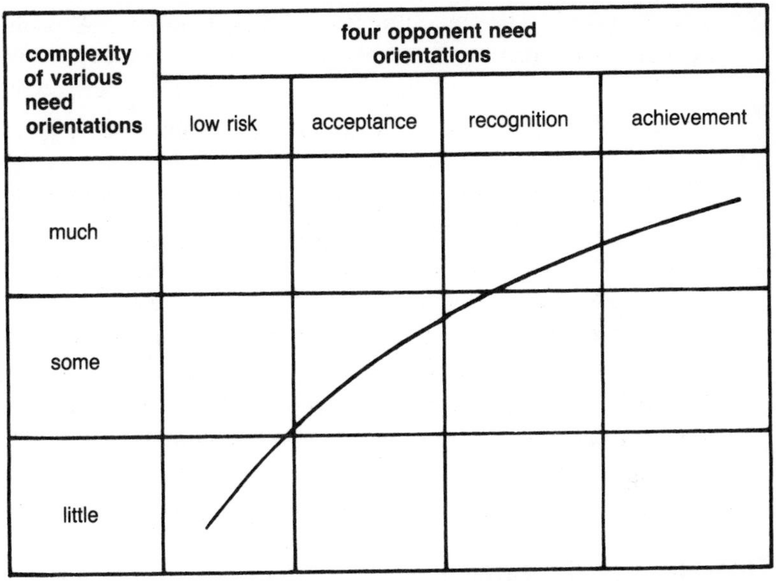

Figure 9-1. Need orientation complexity. (Adapted from A. Maslow.)

need orientation is a minor factor on the influence scene. The style that emerges from the need orientation is a major factor determining the difficulty in influencing an opponent. Styles are described and explored in detail in Chapter 12.

Five Common Wants

All parties in a negotiation want things in addition to meeting their need orientation and attaining their organizational objectives. As a minimum, the negotiator should avoid committing an error on any one of five wants common to most people involved in negotiations. The first three of these are ways in which most people want to be thought of by others. The remaining two are things most people want to experience when dealing with others.

1. Fair: accepting rather than questioning one's intellectual honesty.
2. Competent: downplaying opponent errors rather than causing them to lose face; at the same time, not being gratuitous.
3. Reasonable: accepting rather than suspecting one's motives, except where the evidence is clear to the contrary.
4. Stability: alerting one to changes rather than springing these on them; not destabilizing a situation on purpose.
5. Control: involving one in developing an outcome rather than discounting him as a contributor; treating one on an equal basis.

A disciplined negotiator remains alert to opponent needs.

The Ben Franklin Appeal

How is the appeal to need orientation actually made? An excellent illustration is the precept employed by Ben Franklin for attending to an opponent's need. It is simple and straightforward. Franklin always spoke about his proposal in strong terms of what it offered for his opponent's interest. Franklin enumerated realistic benefits that would accumulate to the opponent. The opponent thereby had real reason for going along with Franklin's proposal. Obviously, Franklin's primary reason for his proposal was that it was in his own side's interest. Rather than explore this facet, he opted to focus on forthcoming opponent benefits. He framed his proposal in terms that the opponent was both familiar with and found comfortable. This gave his proposal added dimension; it gained in meaning.

Example

When the American colonists were battling the British, they required more resources than they could garner on their own. Envoys were sent to all the European countries asking for money, war materials, ships, and even men. All these envoys failed, except Franklin. He convinced the French to help the colonists. His argument was not based on the ethical or moral righteousness of the colonists' stand. It was not predicated on the fact that the colonists were losing, and that their effort was likely doomed without substantial outside aid. Franklin knew sympathy seldom converted to deed. Instead, Franklin harped on the fact that the British had defeated the French repeatedly in Europe and elsewhere. He consistently pushed forward the idea that the British actions were responsible for France's second-rate status in the eyes of many other governments. He talked around the impression, but let the French officials draw the conclusion that France could never achieve the recognition it felt due while the British stayed dominant. Finally, Franklin continually pointed out that British defeat by the colonists could serve to reduce overall British prestige and position. The clear inference was that France was the best candidate to benefit from British loss. France would automatically fill any void left by the British.

The need orientation Franklin perceived as strong enough to get the French to act was recognition. In this instance, it was expressed as pride. Franklin won out by concentrating on the possibility that a single undertaking could regain national pride. It would also elevate France's world-power position. Of course, Franklin's real purpose had nothing to do with the potential benefits to France. Figure 9-2 presents the Franklin model.

Job Conditioning

There is an additional factor to consider when sizing up the opponent from a need standpoint. Most people do other work in addition to negotiating. This other work results in what can be called job conditioning. There are a given set of demands for success in any particular job. These demands provide the job holder with a propensity for either certainty or uncertainty.

People oriented to certainty generally look for and are attracted to propositions having benefits now. They are more interested in abso-

Expressed rationale for the opponent's accepting negotiator's proposal: → → → →	It is in your own and your organization's best interest to accept.	**Dominant Need of Opponent Who Receives Appeal**
	Examples: Situation warrants this outcome.	Achievement
	Gives you competitive edge.	Recognition
	Everyone like us is doing it.	Acceptance
	Safe as the rock of Gibraltar.	Low risk
Unexpressed rationale for the negotiator's proposal: → → →	It is in our own best interest to have this accepted.	**Appeal**
	Examples: Meets our objectives. Will be well perceived. Let us join the group. We give up the least in this instance.	Achievement Recognition Acceptance Low risk

Figure 9-2. The Franklin model. (Source: Sparks Consultants.)

lutes. Typically, these are people trained in such fields as accounting, engineering, and other evaluative disciplines. Similarly, they might have jobs that require them to meet tight specifications or that have exacting standards. Examples are packing parachutes, running patient tests in a hospital laboratory, and making close-tolerance machined parts.

People not concerned with certainty generally look for and are attracted more to benefits-later proposals. They like exploring un-

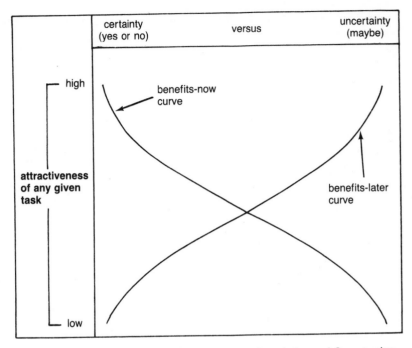

Figure 9-3. Job conditioning model. (Source: *Psychology of Communication and Persuasion,* J.K. Holland.)

chartered areas. These people are often trained in such fields as sales, personnel, and other analytical disciplines. Similarly, they might have jobs that require being comfortable with ambiguities and getting along in less structured situations. Examples are brokering commodities, doing research chemistry, and designing prototypes for appliances.

Depending on his evaluation of opponent job conditioning, the negotiator should emphasize either the benefits-now or the benefits-later aspects in his proposition. He has a better chance of neither turning the opponent off nor of losing him.

Using a compatible frame of reference does not challenge the opponent to mentally change environments. Figure 9-3 shows the job-conditioning model.

Guideline: Discover early an opponent's regular assignment and his training. If possible, identify how he fits in to the formal and informal organizations and assess his position in the power structure.

Control Conditioning

It is important to determine early if an opponent is in a control position in his regular job. The question to answer is "Does this person own or direct capital?" If he does, he is in a control position. He will often be more seasoned by having this type of responsibility. If not, he may likely be more concerned with minutiae, with trifles. He could be circumspect and less flexible. Method is probably more important to him than result.

The important role of power is the subject of the next chapter.

CHAPTER 10

Power

The Lion and the Mouse

A Lion was awakened from sleep by a Mouse running over his face. Rising up angrily, he caught him and was about to kill him, when the Mouse piteously entreated saying: "If you would only spare my life, I would be sure to repay your kindness." The Lion laughed and let him go. It happened shortly after this that the Lion was caught by some hunters, who bound him by strong ropes to the ground. The Mouse recognizing his roar, came up, gnawed the ropes with his teeth, and set him free, exclaiming: "You ridiculed the idea of my ever being able to help you, not expecting to receive from me any repayment of your favor; but now you know that it is possible for even a Mouse to confer benefits on a Lion."

Aesop's Fables

Managing Power Factors

Power factors are always present in any negotiating situation. Their importance ranges from pre-eminent to significant. To perform competently, the negotiator must understand power factors. He must be able to modify their balance between himself and his opponent. What is power? What are its characteristics? What alters the balance of power between two opposing sides?

Complete Power

Complete power can manifest itself in several forms.

1. It is the force permitting the imposition of one position over another, regardless of their relative merits.
2. It is the ability to exert one's will over others, regardless of their relative rank or authority.
3. It is the capacity to influence others to do what they might not ordinarily do in absence of that influence.

The typical outcome of using complete power is in favor of the party exerting it. However, people who use power in an intimidating manner while aggressively pursuing their goals often burn the candle at both ends. They forge agreements that do not hold up when the pressure is removed. They generate hostility in the other party.

Rarely in negotiations will complete power be encountered. If it existed, there probably would be no need for a negotiation. The negotiator can expect to find a state of incomplete power between himself and his opponent. On some points or issues one party usually has more strength than the other and vice versa.

The Six Tasks

There are six tasks that must be mastered by the negotiator in his quest to manage power factors. These are

1. Recognizing power discrepancy.
2. Modifying imbalances.
3. Recognizing risk.
4. Avoiding power-based arguments.
5. Avoiding manipulation.
6. Using logic tools.

Once understood, these tasks can be accomplished in ways beneficial to the negotiating process.

Recognizing Power Discrepancy

The negotiator's first task is recognizing the amount of discrepancy in power between himself and his opponent. This discrepancy can transcend comparative positional strengths and negotiator/opponent skill-level differences. Power discrepancy is difficult to uncover through direct analysis. Instead, it is easier and more sensible to look for the inverse relationship, which is dependency. Four main factors create dependency.

1. *Position:* the reliance on another person or the need for their output to complete one's own tasks or attain one's own goals. For example, the opponent needs the negotiator to complete a deal and vice versa. Position dependency is always present in negotiations. It is modified by either parties' alternatives and their ability to pursue them.
2. *Authority:* the reliance on the authorization or support of another person to move ahead on a project. For instance, the negotiator and opponent must agree to proceed from one issue to another. Authority dependency is always present in negotiations.
3. *Knowledge:* the reliance on another person for information that is required for one's own needs, work, goals, satisfaction, etc. For instance, by furnishing data not previously known by the negotiator, the opponent confirms as fact what was until that time an assumption. Usually, knowledge dependency is present in negotiations.
4. *Affection:* actual limits or imposed self-limits on the sources available to fill one's self-esteem needs. For example, the opponent seeks compliments from the negotiator. Affection dependency is sometimes present in negotiations.

When the negotiator determines the dependency situation, he automatically finds the reciprocal: the extent of the power discrepancy. Figure 10-1 illustrates a typical dependency/power relationship.

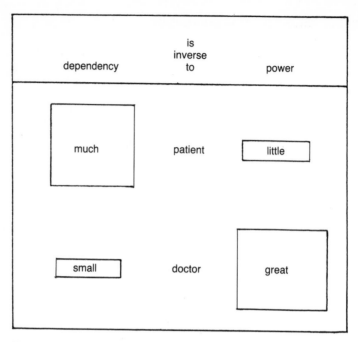

Example: The physician has position, authority, and knowledge vastly exceeding his patient's. This is a common relationship between them. It is very unbalanced.

Figure 10-1. The dependence/power relationship. (Source: *Management and Machiavelli,* A. Jay.)

Modifying Power Imbalances

The second task for the negotiator is modifying existing imbalances in power between himself and his opponent. The merits of each side's position when power is nearly equalized become more important. The negotiator's thorough preparation then provides real strength. If the opponent is also well prepared, the negotiation will progress rapidly. However, observation of many negotiations reveals that some people try purposely to create an imbalance of power in their favor. They feel this is one sure means for attaining their goals.

Four broad changes will modify an existing imbalance of power in a negotiating situation.

1. Change the amount of actual authority the negotiator and/or opponent has to make agreements.

Examples

Expanding or contracting the settlement range available to either party. They may need to refer more or less often to higher authority.

Changing the organizational status and title of either party. This may bring both parties closer to positional parity.

Bringing in new people to replace those already in the negotiation. This has the potential difficulties in information transfer discussed in Chapter 2 and those of adequate preparation described in Chapter 5.

2. Change the agenda.

Examples

Increasing or decreasing the number or types of items that can be considered. Mutually agreeing to extend the negotiation into areas not originally scheduled is one form of this change.

Getting an item included for which the other party is inadequately prepared. Cosmetic changes, such as simply recasting the same items in different form, are not agenda changes.

3. Change the beliefs about or emphasis on the opponent.

Example

The negotiator must understand that his own positional weaknesses are not a reason for assigning or perceiving additional opponent strength. The opponent may not even be aware of the negotiator weaknesses.

4. Change the time available for reaching a settlement.

Examples

The negotiator exercises patience to give the opponent enough time to work out the merits of differing positions.

The negotiator spends extra effort updating his position during recess. Strategy for subsequent meetings is adjusted.

The negotiator maintains strong commitment to his original goals while enduring grinding, wearing discussions.

Risk of Using Power

The third task for the negotiator is recognizing the risk created by the use of power. The employment of power always raises the possibility that whoever is on the receiving end may react unpredictably. Furthermore, abuse through use of power almost always leads to residual damage to the parties' relationship. The assumption that the other party lacks the courage to react to abuse is faulty. It has wrecked lots of negotiations.

Avoiding Use of Power-Based Arguments

The negotiator's fourth task is to avoid using power-based arguments when trying to alter the power distribution. These arguments are used to divert attention from the real issue or point being discussed. Diversion hurts the chances for maintaining clear thinking about the issue or point. Clear thinking requires sticking to the question. There are five general power-based arguments; they should not be used by the negotiator.

1. Arguments of personal abuse that are irrelevant to the point being discussed.

Example
Suggesting an opponent's entire position is undermined by a minor error contained in it. This consists of picking off incorrect information used in support of the opponent's position, but upon which it is not actually dependent.

The negotiator can escape the personal abuse argument being used against himself by ensuring that the evidence used to support his position is relevant.

2. Arguments of absence that attempt to prove a point by asserting that it has never been disproved.

Example

Stating that an opponent's position is untenable because its tenability has never been established.

The negotiator can turn aside the absence argument if used against him. He points out that the apparent absence of something neither proves nor disproves anything. The existence of an absence must actually be determined.

3. Arguments of popularity that are designed to discourage examination of evidence and encourage uncritical acceptance of ideas.

Example

This is the general practice for this industry (popularity for). It just is not done that way by anybody (popularity against).

The negotiator can blunt the popularity argument by pointing out that popular support does not indicate decision soundness. The herd's instinct is not always right.

4. Arguments appealing to stature that are designed to dispense with the need for proof while increasing deference to authority.

Example

Introducing an expert to support or dispute the need for something.

The negotiator can counter the stature argument by providing an expert equally prestigious to refute what the first expert said. He should always check the credentials of expertise claimed by opponents.

5. Arguments of cause and effect that are based on the presumption that if one event comes after another, the second event happened because of the first. This is a fallacy and should be exposed, since subsequent events are not automatically the

result of preceding ones. An opponent may use this argument because he is imprecise in his thinking.

Negotiators should also be aware of the existence of oxymorons. An opponent might describe the negotiator's position as having an "unproductive solution;" or he might suggest getting a "trial concession" from the negotiator to indicate good faith. Oxymorons should be brought to light for what they are: illogical expressions and therefore untenable.

Avoiding Manipulation

The fifth task for the negotiator is to not attempt to manipulate an opponent. It is sometimes tempting for a negotiator to imagine he can discover an opponent's psychological reward system. He could then, theoretically, manipulate the opponent by either giving or withholding rewards. This would provide an edge in power to the negotiator. From a practical context, manipulating someone's reward system is nonsense. First, the discovery of someone else's reward system is difficult even for trained clinicians. Second, the direction the reaction takes to reward receipt or reward deprivation can swing widely. The recipient might move in the giver's desired direction. Just as probable, he might stiffen his resistance to the giver. Rewards management is a poor selection as a technique for altering the balance of power.

Using Logic Tools

The sixth task for a negotiator is to employ tools of logic in support of his win/win approach. There are four tools to use consistently.

1. *Generalization:* projecting from a particular case to a general principle, where that case truly represents that principle. This is inductive reasoning. Negotiators who are adept at learning as they acquire bits of information can use this tool.

Example

An opponent is found to be devious on one point. It is a fair bet that he cannot be trusted too far on anything similar.

2. *Deduction:* reducing a universal situation to an individual case, where that case has characteristics truly representing the universal model. This is deductive reasoning. Negotiators who recognize that success is often a matter of proportion can use this tool.

Example

An opponent has been consistent in meeting his contractural obligations. It is a good bet he will deliver on a particular contract once he agrees to it.

3. *Analogy:* transferring arguments and conflicts from subjects provoking strong feelings to like topics that arouse little emotion. The opponent can look at things in a new way. The chance that high feelings will bring about a negotiating failure is reduced.

Example

An opponent is after an order-cost reduction. He also insists on the same elements that were in the last contract. The negotiator suggests increasing the order size to a total that provides the cost saving desired. Along with this, he suggests not altering the number of individual orders. The opponent views this situation as meeting his demands. The negotiator treats the several orders as one total with different dates.

4. *Syllogism:* identifying that the acceptance of truth for a given premise automatically produces certain conclusions. It would be inconsistent with what has already been admitted for the conclusions not to follow.

Examples

An opponent states that the terms and conditions in the negotiator's document are acceptable. The negotiator must not assume these terms and conditions represent the only ones that will be involved. The correct conclusion is different. The opponent, by omitting words like "inclusive" or "all," has left the door open to introduce additional terms and conditions; usually at his convenience.

The opponent categorizes a particular point as being non-negotiable. The negotiator accepts this stand. Later in the negotiation, another point is brought up similar to the non-negotiable point. By accepting the first exclusion, the negotiator may involuntarily be excluding other items.

The most effective way to deal with power questions is to combine the use of logic tools with changes that modify any imbalance of power. This eliminates the need to resort to other methods that produce questionable results.

The next chapter deals with influencing opponents.

CHAPTER 11

Influencing Opponents

The Wolf and the Sheep

A Wolf, sorely wounded and bitten by dogs, lay sick and maimed in his lair. Being in want of food, he called to a Sheep who was passing, and asked him to fetch some water from a stream flowing close beside him. "For," he said, "if you will bring me drink, I will find means to provide myself with meat." "Yes," said the Sheep, "if I should bring you the draught, you would doubtless make me provide the meat also."

Hypocritical speeches are easily seen through.
Aesop's Fables

The electrical charge in the human brain is maximally 25 watts. Negotiators should try to give messages that require only the wattage necessary for content understanding. This avoids overloading the opponent. If an opponent has low wattage, a real problem is present for the negotiator.

Influencing an opponent to appreciate the negotiator's viewpoint consists of two primary actions:

1. Gaining a high receptivity level.
2. Presenting ideas effectively.

Gaining a High Receptivity Level

The most effective way to get a message across is to deliver it when the opponent is receptive. Receptivity is reached when an opponent both listens and understands. Four actions help the negotiator achieve opponent receptivity. He should

1. Clear static at the conscious level.
2. Employ a positive verbal expression pattern for the subconscious level.
3. Choose and use probes that are applicable.
4. Present ideas properly.

Clearing Static

Static impairs message content from reaching its intended target. Static lowers receptivity at the conscious level. To clear static, first list the types that may be encountered in a particular negotiation. Next, work on those that are identified as reducible. A comprehensive static list is impractical, since each negotiating situation will have a different mix.

The differences between reducible and nonreducible static are illustrated as follows. *Reducible:* Distraction from the noise of typewriters, telephones, and traffic; from terms used (the clearer and simpler, the better); and from climate (comfort and amenities will reduce stress). *Nonreducible:* Opponent biases, personal chemistry between the negotiator and opponent, and non-negotiating vital concerns of the opponent (involving his home life, health, or job).

Static can also be caused by boredom. This is reducible by planning longer negotiating periods first. As total time in the negotiation grows, interest lags. In union negotiations, drawing things out is a frequent tactic. Increasing the frequency of breaks by decreasing the time between them raises attention spans. The attention span falls faster, however, in each successive period. Figure 11-1 illustrates this phenomena.

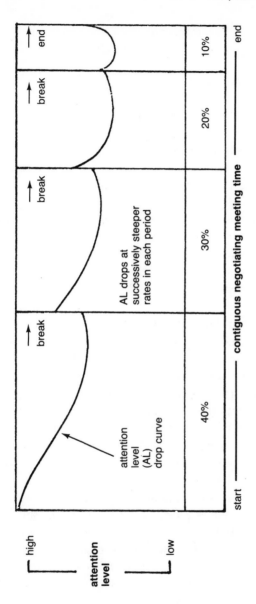

As time grows, interest lags. Increasing the frequency of breaks brings attention back to a higher level. However, it falls faster in each contiguous period. Schedule longer periods first.

Figure 11-1. Scheduling negotiating sessions. (Source: *The Responsive Chord*, T. Schwartz.)

Guideline: Negotiators must guard against boredom and loss of interest, particularly in prolonged negotiations.

Verbal Expression Patterns

A person's verbal expression pattern affects message receptivity at the subconscious level. Expression pattern consists of both positive and negative elements. When the positive elements predominate, listener receptivity is heightened. Positive elements are questions, doubts, uncertainties, and approvals. These demonstrate that the issue being discussed is open to examination of its benefits and arguments. Negative elements are flat assertions and contradictory emotions. These convey that the issue being discussed is closed to examination. They lower listener receptivity. They are counter-productive. The classic phrase showing the effect of a negative expression pattern is "I understood what X said, but I did not like the way he said it."

The negotiator can determine his expression pattern by asking trusted colleagues and friends how he comes across. Assessing responses gives the negotiator a picture of the effect his expression pattern has on opponent receptivity. A precise method for determining expression pattern is to make a verbatum transcript of negotiating sessions. Verbal expressions used by each person are categorized as plus or minus. These are each divided by that person's total expressions. A verbal expression pattern ratio is the result. Very little research has been done in this important area of communication.

A parallel effect of verbal expression patterns happens because people store pieces of data randomly in their subconscious. These data consists of experiences and information. The data can either be positive or negative. When a message is received, it may well trigger one of these stored data pieces. The message receives a plus or minus charge. Its perception by the receiver can be changed, for instance, from a neutral or positive to a minus. This happens independently of the actual intent of the message.

Guideline: Negotiators who are unsure of their opponent's backgrounds, preferences, etc. should avoid discussing subjects not relative to the negotiation; these generally include dress, religion, politics, food, and other personal preference items.

Probes

Probes are questions used by negotiators for one of three purposes: to open or start a discussion, to keep one going, or to track down information.

Start probes are used to get information flowing from the opponent to the negotiator. They have one common characteristic: they cannot be answered by a yes or a no. Very little practice is required to master using start probes. They are a common part of social communication.

Mid probes serve to keep an opponent talking when he has provided incomplete or insufficient information. They too are a part of regular social communication. They require little practice to master.

Using start and mid probes correctly requires concentration. To keep his mind clear, the negotiator should use his regular conversational tone of voice. Attempting special tones, such as inquisitive or solicitous, is a waste of time. Most people cannot successfully use these contrived tones. In trying them, the negotiator risks diverting effort away from content. The listener may also be put-off.

End probes enable the negotiator to get closure or tie things together. Of the three reasons for using probes, closure is paramount. Considerable skill in using end probes is needed for negotiating success. There are two categories of end probes. In one category, the negotiator puts forth a problem or question. He follows this by suggesting a solution or an answer. The solution or answer is stated so that the opponent's response reveals his stand: "We have a demanding timetable for this project, but it can be met. Do you agree?"

In the other category, the negotiator states his impression of what the opponent appears to suggest. He follows this by asking for confirmation. The opponent response provides feedback on the correctness of the negotiator's interpretation: "Your feeling appears to be that progress payments are warranted if option A is selected instead of option B."

End probes deal with more certainty than either start or mid probes, and sometimes with a commitment. They are delivered best when cushioned by a preceding alert. This alert tells the opponent an end probe is coming. It also provides the rationale for it. The best form of alert consists of the negotiator expressing a personal need: "I would like to check my understanding at this time," followed by the end probe; or "Could we take a minute to clear up a point for me?" followed by the end probe. Expressing a personal need takes the edge off the end probe. It removes any inference of shortcoming in the opponent's position. It avoids implied criticism that the opponent is not being candid, as in "You mean to say . . . ."

There are other advantages to effective probing. It helps separate first-level from second-level assumptions, which are described in Chapter 5. It helps when reexamining assumptions made in the planning phase: How well do they hold up in light of data uncovered during the negotiation?

Presenting Ideas

Presenting ideas properly primarily consists of idea spacing, example structuring, repetition, opponent involvement, physical distance, listening, and enlarging the amount of shared information.

Spacing. The mind handles and digests information sequentially and one piece at a time. The rate or speed with which individuals do this varies widely. It is not particularly associated with intelligence. Ideas must be presented with enough space between them to allow a full digestion period. Otherwise a subsequent idea might prematurely push out the idea ahead before it is adequately digested. Alternatively, the idea following may not even gain entry. Too little space is "idea tailgating." The problem for the negotiator is in determining the space needed between ideas for a particular opponent.

Guideline: Leave more digestion space behind presentation of complex ideas and proposals. Leave less space for simpler ones. Learn to read the opponent's eyes. Eyes often mirror the rate and amount of comprehension.

Example

Using examples to reenforce the concepts of complex ideas helps clear away any cobwebs. Well thought-out, preplanned examples are a definite plus. An example with too many parts is compound. The opponent may not be able to follow through to the original concept. This can cause wear out. Wear out leads to rejection of both the example and the idea. It is counterproductive.

Guideline: Use examples that are simpler than the idea they are supposed to clarify or reenforce. Avoid using compound examples, i.e. ones composed of several elements or parts.

Repetition. Applied sparingly, idea repetition is useful in negotiations. Unlike saturation advertising, too much repetition causes throw-off. Throw-off occurs when the idea and its repetitions are purged. The opponent's mind says "Enough," and also "Get out."

Guideline: Limit repetitions whose purpose is to help gain acceptance of ideas to two times. Figure 11-2 presents a negotiation idea repetition model.

Involvement. Participation by an opponent in idea development aids in idea understanding. The idea's acceptability is enhanced. Involvement is accomplished two ways. One way is through the use of directional thinking. This is asking a question whose answer requires application of the data that were presented. It indicates an understanding of what the data mean. The other way is through exploring how something would be accomplished. By enumerating the steps involved, the idea can be seen as workable. Establishing the practicality of a proposal reduces part of the objection or resistance to it.

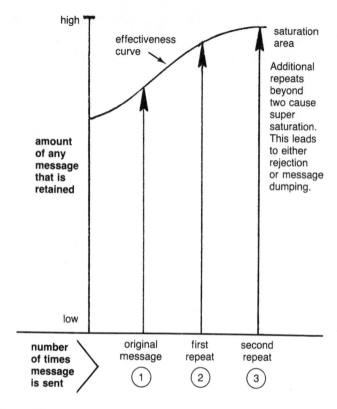

Figure 11-2. Idea repetition model. (Source: *How To Talk with People*, I. Lee.)

Guideline: Involve the opponent in developing inactment steps when exploring the possibility of a desired agreement. Try to do this by skipping temporarily the yes/no part of the discussion. Instead, go directly to "Let us see if this is workable, even though we have not yet agreed to doing it."

Distance. In United States culture, three distances exist that are useful during negotiations. The private zone is from the person to two feet. Getting closer than two feet in negotiations often evokes a defensive or aggressive response. The personal zone is between two and five feet from the opponent. Within that zone, physical proximity tends to emphasize what is said. This is a good technique to use. The social zone is between five and twelve feet. What is said within that zone tends to be deemphasized.

Guideline: Make important points, statements, ideas, and confirmations that are favorable within the personal zone. Make unfavorable positions and rejections from the social zone to reduce their bite. Avoid the private zone in business negotiations.

Listening. Being a good listener has several pluses for a negotiator. Superior listening skill enables one to infer, from what is said, that which is important but is unsaid. It enables one to hear a point of view. This is a critical step to evaluating merits of the opponent's position. Listening helps one avoid using argument-provoking replies. These often happen when what was initially said is not what was hoped for or expected. Listening reduces the chance that a defensive rebuttal, an attempted hard line, or a too early justification of one's own position will be made. Listening enables the negotiator to reflect upon and paraphrase opponent views. He can clarify them. This helps satisfy the opponent that the negotiator understands his side. After that, the opponent should be more attentive to the content of the negotiator's statements. Opponents generally lower their defenses when their side of an issue or point is being discussed. During this time, the negotiator is best served by not using value statements. He should concentrate instead on tangible outcomes.

Listening is often poor because people generally receive little or no adequate listening training. While people do receive training in writing, reading, and speaking, the development of their listening skills is often left to chance. Listening effectively involves hearing both what is said and what is unsaid. To improve his listening, a negotiator should concentrate on judging content, not delivery; withholding judgment until comprehension is complete; identifying the central theme of the speaker; fighting distractions; and weighing evidence in what is said by mentally summarizing it.

Guideline: Fine-tune listening skills. An excellent reference is Rudolph Flesch's *How To Write, Speak & Think More Effectively.*

Information sharing. There is always the question as to who first gives solid information about position or issues. A lot of erroneous ideas persist about the individual who talks first, i.e. at the start of a negotiating session. The most prominent one is that it is a sign of weakness; it gives an advantage to one's opponent, The exact opposite is true for negotiators who plan properly. They include a starting position and ways to introduce it. Being first has two advantages. One, the negotiator is saying to the opponent, "I trust you enough to present some information about my side." The negotiator may even say at the outset of negotiations that he does not mind starting. He also indicates that he expects to get some information after giving some. Two, the negotiator gets to choose what information he exposes as a starter. It should be about something he feels is on both his and the opponent's agendas. He then does not expose his concern with an item not on the opponent's agenda. That mistake would provide the opponent leverage to use when working for something he wants.

In most negotiations an issue common to both sides can be identified during planning and preparation. Figure 11-3 depicts enlarging the area of knowledge shared by the negotiator and opponent in order to reach an agreement productively. This area of shared knowledge is termed the Arena. It is often worthwhile to restate things at the outset of a negotiation. This is one way to ascertain whether or not the Arena is already of sufficient size to accomplish the negotiation. If it is, one would not divulge any data outside the Arena. There would be no need to explore more data than are needed to resolve the issues. When a solution has been reached, the negotiator must stop, even though he has not used all his prepared data. Negotiators can always evaluate the adequacy of their preparation based on whether or not they have data left over, unused. If so, preparation was adequate. This contrasts to the situation where all data were used. It is not possible to know what the result might have been if more data were available.

Guideline: Some negotiating advantage is gained and the relationship with the opponent is improved by talking first. Develop an

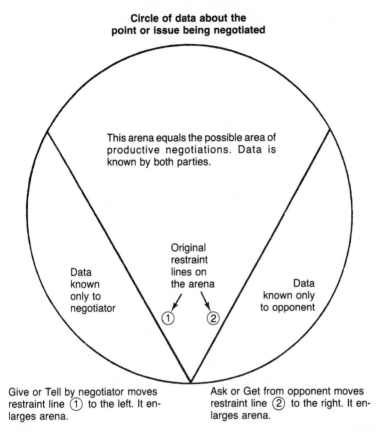

Circle of data about the point or issue being negotiated

This arena equals the possible area of productive negotiations. Data is known by both parties.

Original restraint lines on the arena

Data known only to negotiator

① ②

Data known only to opponent

Give or Tell by negotiator moves restraint line ① to the left. It enlarges arena.

Ask or Get from opponent moves restraint line ② to the right. It enlarges arena.

Figure 11-3. Enlarging the Arena. (Source: *The Johari Window,* J. Hall.)

economy of judgment; know when to stop. Accept the inefficiency of overpreparation as a necessary step in achieving effectiveness.

Guideline: In tense situations, a negotiator should be aware of when to not say anything. This is often effective in reducing tension, in "cooling" things.

Negotiations Conduct: Summary

Negotiators do better when they can conceptualize about conflict as it evolves during the negotiation. They are less apt to be intimidated when armed with the twin protectors—personal and organizational. Recognizing opponent need orientation enables the negotiator to influence opponents more. Negotiators need skill to achieve and maintain a healthy balance in power between themselves and their opponents. Logic tools are very useful. When opponent receptivity is gained and held, negotiators are more successful.

Negotiators who have the following three abilities can do these things just described, and they will be more productive.

Task performance is the ability to plan and to think things through analytically; it is also a combination of persistence and competitiveness backed by the stamina to remain that way.

Thought process is the ability to think clearly under pressure and to maintain a sense of realism. It is having common sense and judgment so that the time to take a particular action will be identified correctly. It includes learning from errors and not repeating them. Judgment is one of the most critical elements for success in negotiations. People who have it, find it grows with age and experience. Those without much of it seem unable to learn it.

Several times during even brief negotiations, one must decide to act or not act or to not act prematurely; balance introspection and extroversion; and know when to press on with one's own conviction. For example, a negotiator who fails to identify when to risk deadlock, tends to do less well after that point in the negotiation. People selected to negotiate should be those who have been observed to have judgment. Unfortunately, judgment is a subject that is yet to receive sufficient scientific investigation.

Thought process is also the ability to arrange things in such a way as to see all the possibilities of what is being presented. Thinking in diagrammatical terms helps. For instance, the negotiator must be able to determine whether two statements are contradictory, i.e., cannot be true together. The statements "at least some A's and B's" and "no A's are B's" might be involved in a negotiation as representing possible agreements. The first statement has at least four representations: A and B in overlapping circles, A and B in the same circle, and A in a smaller circle within a large B circle and vice versa. However, the second statement has only one representation: two independent, i.e. nonconnected, circles, one A and one B. Therefore both statements could not be true together. By determining this, the negotiator can avoid agreeing to something that will undoubtedly evolve into a problem later when the contradiction surfaces.

Diagrammatic thinking also helps when a negotiator needs to determine whether a possibility is exclusive, exhaustive, both exclusive and exhaustive, or neither exclusive nor exhaustive. If A and B are exclusive, they do not overlap in any way, but may not cover every possibility. If they are exhaustive, they cover every possibility in the circumstance under review, but may not be exclusive of one another. If they are both exclusive and exhaustive, they cover every possibility but do no overlap. If they are neither exclusive nor exhaustive, they overlap and do not cover every possibility.

Socializing is the ability to be comfortable with others, even in stressful situations. It is a combination of self-control and personal honesty that provides personal worth. High personal worth is necessary if a negotiator is to avoid being ridden by events or opponents.

Negotiators who are often successful realize that being a perfectionist reaps imperfection. Their aim is not to get everything. Instead, when a genuine agreement has been reached on one point they go on to another.

The next part of this book deals with opponent styles, strategies, and tactics. It includes counteractions the negotiator can take and guides for handling stylistic opponents.

Part IV

Dealing with Opponent Styles, Strategies, and Tactics

Dealing with Opponent Styles, Strategies, and Tactics: Introduction

Many people negotiate from a stylistic base rather than from an issue orientation. By recognizing opponent stylism, negotiators can anticipate the actions that are part of it. Opponents usually have a primary style and at least one, sometimes two, secondary styles. Part IV examines the opponent's primary and secondary styles. It enumerates the steps negotiators should consider when dealing with them.

Stylistic opponents involuntarily provide the negotiator a competitive edge. He can adopt strategies which blunt or negate the strength of a particular style. Once the stylistic approach and attendant strategies are expended, the opponent is faced with working the issue. The negotiator's issue preparation then puts the opponent at some disadvantage. Preparing around the issues is more successful than counting on style. However, style can be an effective support to issue orientation. That is its rightful use.

There are various ways to look at style. The approach used here is based on the personality model developed by Carl Jung. It is both practical and easy to understand. Jung was a Swiss psychiatrist. Although a contemporary and friend of Sigmund Freud, he differed with him. Jung emphasized drives that direct one's actions instead of emphasizing one's past sexual development. Jung's model is altered to fit the subject of stylistic opponents. This revised model is a convenience for the negotiator. The tactics generally used in, but not exclusive to, each style are discussed. Methods for effectively dealing with each style accompany its description.

CHAPTER 12

Opponent Styles

The Three Tradesmen

A Great City was besieged, and its inhabitants were called together to consider the best means of protecting it from the enemy. A Bricklayer earnestly recommended bricks as affording the best material for an effective resistance. A Carpenter, with equal enthusiasm, proposed timber as a preferable method of defense. Upon which a Currier stood up and said, "Sirs, I differ from you altogether; there is no material equal to a covering of hides; and nothing so good as leather."

Every man for himself.
Aesop's Fables

The Four Opponent Styles

There are four primary styles used by non-issue oriented opponents. Each style is based on a set of assumptions. Usually two drives (out of a set of four) act in concert to create this set of assumptions about the other party. The drives are as follows:

1. *Control:* the drive to dominate and rule others; the belief in the correctness of direct, unbridled rivalry.

123

2. *Disregard:* the drive to discount others; the belief that passive endurance and extreme attention to detail are of the highest importance.
3. *Deference:* the drive to let others take the lead; the belief that disinterest or patience have the most value.
4. *Trust:* the drive to include others as working partners; the belief that collaboration is best.

Figure 12-1 depicts how these forces blend to produce the four stylistic opponents. The styles and assumptions underlying each are:

1. *Restrictive:* control combines with disregard to form the assumption that negotiators must be forced to settle. They are automatically going to be uncooperative. This is the way things are. These opponents expect people to act in their own interest in whatever way is needed. The only outcomes acceptable to the restrictive-style opponent are getting a win or deadlocking.
2. *Elusive:* disregard combines with deference to form the assumption that negotiators must be avoided or kept remote. They represent a source of trouble; they will do what they feel like doing. The perception is that people cannot be influenced by the actions of others. It is useless to try to deal on a personal level. It is better to concentrate on procedures and rules. The overriding goal of the elusive-style opponent is to survive the negotiation. Maintaining the status quo is next in importance. Accomplishing any results is tertiary.
3. *Friendly:* deference and trust combine to form the assumption that negotiators are usually cooperative, even sympathetic. They are influenced by good sportsmanship. There are, of course, competitive situations. If one takes a larger view while avoiding detail and nitpicking, things can be sketched out. The main goal of the friendly-style opponent is maintaining the relationship with the negotiator. This is irrespective of whether or not anything of substance is achieved.
4. *Confrontive:* trust and control combine to form the assumption that negotiators are after fairness. They appreciate the need to

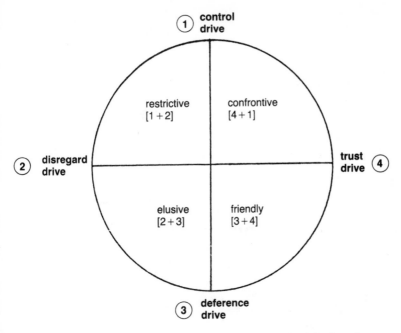

Figure 12-1. Opponent styles. (Source: Work of C. Jung.)

contest the issues while mutually working with one another as a means of arriving at solid agreement. The view is that people will collaborate rather than obstruct if that option is available. People will be objective if they are not treated subjectively. The goal of the confrontive-style opponent is the best overall agreement under the circumstances. It should be one heavily backed by merit and mutual commitment to seeing it enacted.

Figure 12-2 shows how these styles relate to the need orientations described in Chapter 9.

Style Similarities

The restrictive and confrontive styles are initiators, while the elusive and friendly styles are mostly reactive. Restrictive-style

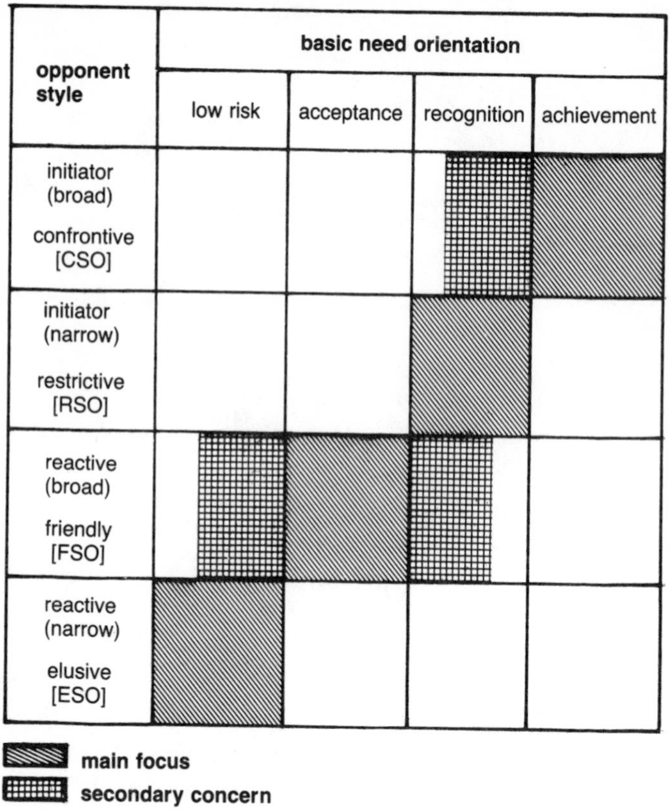

opponent style	basic need orientation			
	low risk	acceptance	recognition	achievement
initiator (broad) confrontive [CSO]			▓ secondary	▓ main focus
initiator (narrow) restrictive [RSO]			▓ main focus	
reactive (broad) friendly [FSO]	▓ secondary	▓ main focus	▓ secondary	
reactive (narrow) elusive [ESO]	▓ main focus			

▓ main focus
▓ secondary concern

Figure 12-2. Opponent styles matched with need orientation. (Source: Works of A. Maslow and C. Jung.)

opponents and confrontive-style opponents have the higher number of settlements. However, commitment to agreement with a restrictive-style opponent is often less than that given to a confrontive-style opponent. This is because the tactics used by restrictive-style opponents usually leave a bad taste with the other party. This is true even when the agreement reached is largely fair. When the agreement is lopsided toward the restrictive-style opponent, the bad taste converts to active hostility. The agreement has a good chance of unraveling in some ways. Possibly, it will abort totally. Restrictive-style opponents employ tactics representing the strategies of force and intimidation. Commitments to an agreement with confrontive-style opponents tend to be the firmest, to hold up the longest, and to have the best chances for completion.

Elusive-style opponents and friendly-style opponents are less productive than the other two styles. This is because they concentrate on things other than getting agreements. The focuses are on survival by the elusive-style opponent, and on relationship maintenance by the friendly-style opponent. Commitment to any agreement made with elusive-style opponents is especially tenuous. Negotiating with an elusive-style opponent is boring, taxing, and, in general, an unrewarding experience. It is like being run over by a flock of stampeding sheep. It takes forever. The commitment to agreement reached with a friendly-style opponent is dominated by social aspects rather than by issue merit. In some cases that may be sufficient. It is still less desirable than settlements hammered out through contention and confrontation.

Each style has a single application that is optimum; it is also different from the others.

Restrictive appears sensible when the issue is a "must settle," involves high stakes, or involves a terminal conflict. *Elusive* has merit when the issue is routine, when it involves heavy detail requiring painstaking review, or when other factors, such as conforming to policy, take precedence over the need for settlement. *Friendly* is applicable when the issue requires exuberance, enthusiasm, diplomacy, and tact, such as smoothing ruffled feelings or where detail is not critical. *Confrontation* is best when the issue is a "must settle," involves high stakes, or involves a contentious conflict.

Need For Flexibility

The different optimal applications for the four styles increase the need for negotiator flexibility. On the one hand, he must accommodate the opponent style. At the same time, he tries to act in a way complementary to each point or issue. By doing so, his opponents must work harder to keep up. They cannot predevelop a strategy based on the predictability of the negotiator's style. Being consistent in a negotiating style is as harmful as being inconsistent in a management style.

Negotiators must realize that while categorizing an opponent's style is very helpful, overreliance on categorization is dangerous. People do not often fit into neat categories, even though they may rely on a stylistic approach more heavily when negotiating.

The next chapter discusses stylistic-based tactics, counters to them, and options for handling opponents.

CHAPTER 13

Stylistic-Based Tactics and Counters

The Ass and His Shadow

A Traveler hired an Ass to convey him to a distant place. The day being intensely hot, and the sun shining in its strength, the Traveler stopped to rest, and sought shelter from the heat under the Shadow of the Ass. As this afforded the only protection for one, and as the Traveler and the owner of the Ass both claimed it, a violent dispute arose between them as to which of them had the right to the Shadow. The Traveler asserted that he had, with the hire of the Ass, hired his Shadow also. The quarrel proceeded from words to blows, and while the men fought, the Ass galloped off.

In quarreling about the shadow we often lose the substance.
Aesop's Fables

Stylistic-Based Tactics

Tactics are the actions through which strategy is enacted. Each style of opponent uses tactics that are based on its assumptions about the other party. Some of the same tactics are used with different styles. The forms in which each tactic appears are numerous. Only the central tactic is described here.

Restrictive-Style Opponent Tactics

The tactics used by restrictive-style opponents are characterized by coercion, fear, and threat.

Deputy. The restrictive-style opponent claims limited authority. This is an attempt to make the negotiator more restrained in his demands. The opponent also uses this tactic to simulate the need to refer to higher authority. He actually seeks time to determine and evaluate the negotiator's position without revealing too much of his own.

Deputies are a fact in some negotiations, a sham in others. The outset of the negotiation is the best place to minimize the effect of this tactic. The negotiator informs his opponent that he will outline his own authority limits—in as much detail as policy permits. He then expects the opponent to do the same. If the opponent agrees, the negotiator proceeds. If not, the indication is that the opponent will try the deputy tactic.

Diminish. A restrictive-style opponent having a weaker position for an issue compared to the negotiator's tries to gain parity. He applies negative but unrelated descriptions to the negotiator's position. This false characterization is designed to reduce the negotiator's positional strength.

Diminution invokes the argument that unpopular things are automatically not good. It is countered by letting the opponent work through his gambit, then insisting on returning to the issue's merits. Argument about the validity of the trumped-up negative uses up time. It only serves to deplete the negotiator's energies.

Irrevocable. Restrictive-style opponents often attempt to go around negotiators to other, probably higher, levels within their organization. They present the negotiators with such statements as "The vice president said we should get your signature and go forward on this," or "Your operating people want this now, so let's get the paperwork out of the way.'' The purpose of this tactic is to intimidate the negotiator. It tries to by-pass an examination of the issue.

Irrevocable is an appeal to higher authority. It can be handled one of two ways, depending on the climate at the negotiator's organization. He can simply refuse to go forward. He tells the opponent to recontact the other person(s) and obtain written authorization backing up what the opponent claims. Alternatively, he can put the opponent in limbo while checking with the other party in his organization. This second course should be handled with care. It contains the risk that the negotiator and the other party in his organization might end up in a conflict. That just might be the opponent's goal. Incidentally, if what the opponent claims is true, the negotiator had better get his duties defined. More opponents might discover he can be neutralized or by-passed so easily.

Startle. The restrictive-style opponent takes an action without informing the negotiator. Perhaps he invites a competitor to the negotiation. He might move the physical site in the midst of the discussion. The purpose of startle is to destabilize the negotiator's thinking; divert it from the issue.

Startles cannot always be avoided. The counter, however, should be to make the startle cost the opponent something. The easiest and most readable cost is delay. In effect it says to the opponent, "Everytime you pull a startle, it may well involve lengthening the negotiation.'' This cost is also borne by the negotiator. It is, however, a better way than arguing about the startle or indicating that it cannot be justified. Arguing here uses up one's energies for a non-issue. Depleting the negotiator's energy might be a purpose behind the tactic. The delay offers the negotiator time to assess the startle and intelligently plot a course of action.

Negotiators should not automatically assume evil motives when a startle occurs. Instead, negotiators should first examine the facts and background and then make a judgment. Is this an intentional tactic or is it unintentional? These four tactics just described are not poor because they may be morally questionable. They are less useful because they do not lead or contribute to genuine settlement. They are less effective because they add no element of longevity to the outcome. RSOs do use a tactic which has beneficial qualities. Like most tactics that are effective, this one has no counter. If it works, its use cannot be proved by the other party.

Reunion. A restrictive-style opponent, if he knows with certainty where the negotiator stands on a particular point or issue, can take a plausible position somewhat away from that point. The negotiator's position, in this case, is actually acceptable to the restrictive-style opponent. The restrictive-style opponent then lets the negotiator move him back to the original position; a seeming concession for the negotiator.

The restrictive style opponent has two advantages from a reunion that works. He is where he wanted to be and he has accepted through negotiation a position that was originally acceptable. He has seemingly made a concession to the negotiator who now owes the restrictive-style opponent a concession, quid pro quo.

Example

The president of a company knew that his principal customer group was holding an important industry coordinating meeting. He discovered one decision in advance of any formal announcement. The group had decided to insist on higher quality standards from suppliers. He instructed his marketing and engineering executives to develop costs on these unpublished, new standards. The data showed the standards were well within his company's current capability. The new standards would in fact benefit the company's products by improving their performance. The president immediately announced a product improvement program in personal letters to high-level customer executives. The program exceeded the new industry standards. This was identifiable by those receiving the letters. The customer executives could deduce that the standards the supplier described signified a substantial price increase. Customer group representatives convinced the supplier to lower its announced product goals to the new industry specifications. They now became more supportive for placing orders at this particular company. It had not upset their industry group plans, and a material increase in sales took place. It was attributable to the supplier president's reunion strategy.

Restrictive-Style Opponent Behavior

Restrictive-style opponents strive to gain any advantage possible. They interpret situations in a way that places them in a favorable light. Restrictive-style opponents talk much and listen little. They use facts to gain a surrender. They adopt fixed positions while bulldozing ahead over the other party. Generally, the restrictive-style opponent is hard working, aggressive, and opinionated. He is most interested in negotiations that will raise his esteem, help his personal progress. What the restrictive-style opponent has failed to learn is that success does not always come from succeeding. There are specific steps the negotiator should take when dealing with a restrictive-style opponent.

1. Let him vent his negative emotions; this is his standard opening approach.
2. Do not argue directly: this increases his combative bent; it confirms his feeling that the negotiator is an enemy to be vanquished.
3. Probe flat assertions or easy yeses; distinguish between them as expressions of his comprehension versus his agreement. This also checks progress and tacks things down as the negotiation moves along.
4. Use facts and provide details; he responds to these and appreciates hard information.
5. Be firm and demonstrate resolve; any sign of weakness heightens his hunger for a kill.
6. Emphasize the benefits from the negotiator proposal that appeal to his need orientation of power, esteem, and independence.

Elusive-Style Opponent Tactics

Tactics used by an elusive-style opponent focus on avoidance. Therefore, delay and procrastination characterize them.

Retire. The elusive-style opponent gives the impression that he is backing away or is in a subordinate position. This is to lull the negotiator into overconfidence. He can expend time, effort, and energy fruitlessly. Then the elusive-style opponent starts at the beginning as though no progress has ever been made.

The counter to retire is to not let it happen at all. Negotiators should summarize at appropriate times as they progress. The elusive-style opponent may not agree that an item is settled. He can be confronted with the need to agree or disagree that it has been explored adequately. This ties-off that part of the discussion as completed, before going on to the next point. It avoids or at least reduces the exasperating rehashing on which elusive-style opponents thrive.

Specimen. An elusive-style opponent often presents selective supporting information quantitatively arranged. He makes the assumption that others will accept it as accurately representing the total of things. This includes the use of quasi-quantified data, pictorial representations instead of graphs, percentages instead of actual numbers, etc. The elusive-style opponent sometimes presents excessive detail from which the specimen was drawn. This is often an attempt to obscure the absence of specific data in sufficient quantity.

The counter to specimen is to express interest in the back-up information. It should be evaluated by the negotiator for whether or not it truly represents the specimen. Technical knowledge may be required, especially where statistical methods are used. Valid statistical methods can be used for the wrong application to get a desired answer.

Virtue. An elusive-style opponent will sometimes be in an obvious weak position vis-à-vis the negotiator. He then assigns qualities to his position in an attempt to gain parity. He hopes to achieve a halo effect. Virtue is the opposite of diminish. It has a better chance of succeeding because it uses positive expressions.

Virtue is best countered by forbearance or, if fitting, humor. The true value of the weaker case is not changed by putting it in a better wrapper. The negotiator should insist on returning to the facts.

Many elusive-style opponent tactics can cause a negotiator to undergo deep frustration. They result in inordinately drawing out the time needed for resolution without adding to its quality. This is true for even minor points. Elusive-style opponents do use a tactic that can be beneficial. Although identifiable, there is no counter to it.

Equanimity. Sometimes anger or impetuous behavior seems justified, as in the case of an attack on one's personal honesty. The greater benefit may be in withholding any overt reaction. Patience may be misjudged as representing indecision. However, it provides the elusive-style opponent time to reflect and measure his response with less emotional influence. Acquiring equanimity is often the result of experience. Its user demonstrates that he has high self-governance and is less subject to impulsiveness.

Elusive-Style Opponent Behavior

Elusive-style opponents seek to survive through opting for perfection. They repress from conscious thought anything repugnant to themselves. They are superficial, talk little and listen little. They are most comfortable in neutral gear. What the elusive-style opponent has not learned is that negotiation is not entirely a numbers activity. Generally, the elusive-style opponent is a plodder, a loner, moody, and works by the book. While somewhat meek, he compensates by being intense. ESOs are most interested in negotiations that are routine and have a known expectation. The negotiator can take specific steps that help deal with an elusive-style opponent.

1. Behave reassuringly and move ahead slowly; this establishes trust and it recognizes his inherent reticence and suspicion.
2. Do not talk too much or too long; this reduces his opportunity to fade away or mentally bail out.
3. Use lots of detail while keeping him involved in exploring its meaning; he likes to get into all the corners.
4. Avoid exploiting his passiveness; his behavior might alter radically.
5. Guide the forward progress constantly; any movement forward will not likely be at his initiation.
6. Emphasize the benefits that appeal to his single consuming need orientation—the absence of risks, i.e. security and safety.

Friendly-Style Opponent Tactics

The friendly-style opponent uses tactics that emphasize a minimal number of goals, easy achievement, and amicability.

Crisscross. This tactic has two dimensions. First, one point or issue is randomly subdivided. It is presented as several items, disconnected and nonadjacent. The negotiator must pull the entity back together and get the friendly-style opponent to accept its integrity. Second, a number of superficial items are introduced that should not be on the agenda. This attempts to disguise the few issues important to the friendly-style opponent.

Crisscross is difficult to deal with, since it has an element of randomness. The negotiator must sort through the muck to find the pearl. The best counter to crisscross is patience coupled with constant, evenly applied pressure on the friendly-style opponent to move ahead. The need for progress furnishes the rationale for reconstituting fragmented issues and scrubbing junk cargo, while sticking to priorities.

Ganging. The friendly-style opponent often tries to enlist the aid of others, even the negotiator, in making his case. The others may not even be involved in the negotiation. His action is based on the erroneous premise that everyone else is as empathetic as he.

Ganging, like crisscross, has an element of randomness that causes difficulty. It seldom brings relevant analysis to bear on the issue. Questioning the relevance of someone else's opinion draws the negotiator off the central question. The better counter to ganging is forbearance. The negotiator rejects the irrelevancies by simply ignoring them.

Synthetic limits. Placing synthetic limits on what can and cannot be accomplished has a dual attraction for friendly-style opponents. First, it tends to show progress to be more than is actually made. Progress is measured against a smaller total, one constrained by the synthetic limits. Second, it downplays any risk that might emerge from the creative problem-solving required of complex issues. That process requires too much effort.

Synthetic limits are expressed in the same terms as real ones—money, time, space, authority, etc. The negotiator should, as a general rule, probe all limits expressed by the opponent. He should challenge those that appear to be unsubstantiated hindrances. The challenge might be in the form of asking for confirmation of the source for the limits. For friendly-style opponents, polite skepticism or patience is usually enough of a reaction. Then the negotiator should push ahead as though the synthetic limits had not been put forth.

Friendly-Style Opponent Behavior

Friendly-style opponents also make ample use of reunion. They look at the positive side of something. They talk much and listen only partially. The friendly-style opponent meanders and will not stick to even his own points. He often interjects unrelated social issues into the negotiation. His is the least competitive of the four styles.

Typically, the friendly-style opponent is charming, a cajoler, and an attractive personality. He is interested in negotiation matters involving talking versus doing. The "big picture" viewpoint predominates with him. Friendly-style opponents have not learned that the fear of harming or losing a relationship can take the joy out of completing a negotiation successfully. There are specific actions that help when confronted with friendly-style opponents.

1. Keep him on track, but give him room to wander, since he lacks self-discipline. Avoid introducing distractions, since enough occur naturally.
2. Uncover unspoken disagreements and probe easy yeses; he avoids being candid in an attempt to not hurt anyone else's feelings. His actual stand must be exposed and dealt with, but gently.
3. Avoid inundating him with facts; he combines the written with the verbal, and he tunes out if too much data overload his circuit.
4. Avoid exploiting his good fellowship; his behavior might alter radically.
5. Guide the forward progress constantly, he accepts moderate direction.
6. Emphasize the benefits that appeal to his need orientation, which is anything positive.

Confrontive-Style Opponent Tactics

The confrontive-style opponent uses tactics that combine collaboration and confrontation while emphasizing negotiator involvement.

Real limits. The confrontive-style opponent attempts to define and establish mutually recognizable limits that exist for both parties. His twin purposes are to move the negotiations along and to block out unnecessary items. This tactic can benefit the negotiator who is well prepared. He must exercise care to not be put into a position of excluding items he wants on the agenda.

The other tactics used most often by the confrontive style opponent—equanimity, reunion, and virtue—have already been described.

Confrontive-Style Opponent Behavior

Confrontive-style opponents are very competitive. They have both the endurance and exuberance of ideas to keep at it. They usually present their positions clearly and listen attentively. While the confrontive-style opponent is driving and aggressive, he is also supportive of others. He will consider trying new approaches. He is most interested in negotiations having risks, innovations, and challenges to creativity. He believes that agreements are possible where both sides share in the winning, but not necessarily equally. What the confrontive-style opponent has not learned is that one's best skills can sometimes become their greatest handicap. There are specific actions a negotiator should execute when confronted with a confrontive-style opponent.

1. Anticipate any weaknesses in negotiator data and be prepared to do something about them; confrontive-style opponents are methodical enough to uncover most weaknesses in the other party's position.
2. Check continually his understanding; monitor the pace, since he moves along quickly and might carry the negotiator into unwanted areas.
3. Use quantity of data where available; he responds to this.
4. Avoid overstating or being imprecise about benefits; he will attack at any hint of a snow job.
5. Demonstrate the use of preparation and planning; he respects and responds favorably to these.
6. Emphasize benefits that appeal to his need orientations of innovation, mutuality, and interdependence.

Tactic and Style(s) Often Using it	Primary Argument Appeal			
	Personal Abuse	Absence of Proof	Popularity	Stature (Authoritative Source or Method)
Deputy [RSO]		✓		
Diminish [RSO]			✓	
Irrevocable [RSO]	✓			
Startle [RSO]	✓			
Retire [ESO]		✓		
Specimen [ESO]				
Virtue [ESO/CSO]				✓
Crisscross [FSO]			✓	
Ganging [FSO]				✓
Synthetic Limits [FSO]			✓	
				✓

Tactics not appealing to a primary argument:

$$\text{Reunion} \begin{bmatrix} \text{RSO} \\ \text{FSO} \\ \text{CSO} \end{bmatrix}$$

$$\text{Equanimity} \begin{bmatrix} \text{ESO} \\ \text{CSO} \end{bmatrix}$$

Real Limits [CSO]

Figure 13-1. Tactics related to primary argument appeal. (Source: Sparks Consultants.)

The tactics of these four opponent styles are tied back to their primary argument appeal in Figure 13-1 (see "Primary Argument Appeal," Chapter 10).

Guidelines for Dealing with All Opponents

Negotiators should hold to four guidelines when working with all opponents. These apply regardless of opponent style.

1. Let the opponent behave naturally. Do not try to manipulate opponent behavior. Instead, adjust as much as possible to

complement the opponent style. Do not add stress to the negotiation. Stress only impairs good judgment.

2. Utilize the opponent's value system to increase receptivity. Remember Ben Franklin's way. Speak of benefits to the opponent interest rather than the logic of why a proposal is worthwhile. The benefits must be expressed in an acceptable context. They must coincide with the direction in which the opponent leans (benefits now versus benefits later) and the interest dominating his attention (power or pride or greed or whatever). These two factors must be balanced with the primary need orientation of the opponent.

3. Guide the opponent to the conclusion desired, but let him state that conclusion, the realization of it. This sets his acceptance level higher than it would be otherwise. However, this is the most difficult guideline. Whether or not an opponent has the ability to draw the conclusion is not always obvious. If he lacks that ability, a lot of time will be spent for no useful purpose.

4. Avoid the animal urge to dominate a seemingly weak opponent. Weakness can be feigned. Reticence can be mistaken for weakness. Style, like behavior, can swing quickly. A tiger might be unleashed; the negotiation can become unnecessarily complicated.

The next chapter explores secondary styles and some of the influences of culture on style.

CHAPTER 14

Style Movement

The Cat and Venus

A Cat fell in love with a handsome young man, and entreated Venus to change her into the form of a woman. Venus consented to her request and transformed her into a beautiful damsal, so that the youth saw her and loved her, and took her home as his bride. While the two were reclining in their chamber, Venus wishing to discover if the Cat in her change of shape had also altered her habits of life, let down a mouse in the middle of the room. The Cat, quite forgetting her present condition, started from the couch and pursued the mouse, wishing to eat it. Venus was much disappointed and again caused her to return to her former shape.

Nature exceeds nurture.
Aesop's Fables

Secondary Styles

Opponents seldom stay with their primary style throughout a negotiation, although they often return to it several times. There are three causes which initiate negotiating style change—natural, directive, and reactive.

Natural

Natural cause can be likened to water flowing down its available trench. The past experience and personal makeup of the opponent combine to shift his style. The action is subconscious. Typically, the movement is toward less trust. Negotiators must be careful to avoid any action that will activate this movement. When an opponent's trust is reduced, the negotiation becomes more difficult. When natural cause alters opponent style, great skill coupled with patience is necessary to modify the resulting secondary style. Part A of Figure 14-1 depicts style change due to natural cause.

Directive

Directive cause can be seen as purposely altering the flow of water. The opponent alters his primary style for reasons of expediency or in a real attempt to achieve a complementary style mix with the negotiator. The action is planned. It is conscious. Directive cause is largely choice and therefore can sometimes be influenced. This change is shown in Part B of Figure 14-1. Very seldom does anyone purposely adopt the elusive style. It is simply too tedious and unrewarding for most people.

Reactive

Reactive cause occurs as a result of two tandem actions. First, the negotiator in some way effectively blocks the opponent from reaching his objective. The opponent bounces off the block to a decision point. He then has three options. He can

1. Attack the block in an attempt to breach it and reach his original goal.
2. Retreat to a deadlock or actually abort the negotiation and go elsewhere.
3. Seek an alternative goal or a modification of the original one that offers a better chance of becoming an agreement.

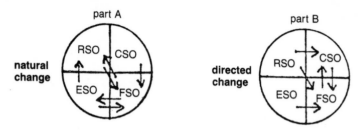

Figure 14-1. Secondary style. (Source: Work of C. Jung.)

Second, the negotiator pushes the opponent before he has time to select an action from the three options above. This indicates a lack of discipline on the negotiator's part. Crowding the opponent in this way is a mistake. He generally reacts by selecting either option one, attack, or two, abort. The third option is excluded by pushing the opponent at the wrong time. This option is probably the most favorable for the negotiator. Figure 14-2 depicts the reactive cause. Since the opponent selects his option, reactive cause can usually be influenced.

Guideline: The briefer the negotiation time, the less likely that significant style shifts will take place to compound the negotiator's work.

Guideline: In any negotiation, opponents will generally evidence at least one secondary style attributable to cause. The negotiator should remember this action when planning future negotiations with the same opponent.

Cultural Influences on Styles

Many of the techniques already discussed apply to negotiating with people from other cultures.

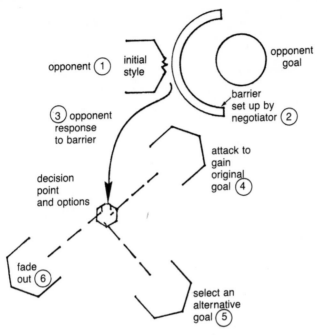

Figure 14-2. Reactive change. (Source: *Flights, Games and Debates*, A. Rapoport.)

There are six important areas for analysis when negotiating with other cultures in addition to the issues.

1. *Sensitivity:* what is opponent expectation regarding rank, age, and protocol? Answers to these questions avoid annoying the opponent unnecessarily.
2. *Authority:* how much routine and precedence has the opponent emphasized as being required to govern the negotiation? The

answer to this question reveals the authority of the opponent. The narrower the authority, the more he depends on structure. The narrower the authority, the more often he will need to consult with his organization.

3. *Rivalries:* how much internecine arguing is there within the opponent organization? The more rivalry, the more the negotiator must use care to avoid being caught in the middle. Internal rival factions will join to attack outsiders.

4. *Opponent support:* what circumstances are evident about support from the opponent organization? Do major slip-ups occur often? Is carelessness obvious? etc. Answers to these questions point the way to the reason for seemingly uncalled for cancellations and postponements.

5. *Personal ties:* does the opponent make it especially difficult to cultivate personal relations with him? This is generally a sign of heavy reliance on structure. Position and rank are more important than individual characteristics. The trust that develops in this climate centers on job positions or organizations rather than on individuals.

6. *Details:* what is the opponent emphasis regarding detail in the final agreement? How does the emphasis on agreement detail or lack of it compare with the emphasis on details in guarantees? Is the emphasis greater, equal, or less? To illustrate, the opponent might seek substantial detail in the final agreement. If he carries this action to the guarantees, such as warranties, a consistent approach is evident. However, the opponent might seek to keep guarantees general. In that case, the negotiator can then conclude that the opponent will make liberal interpretations regarding warranties, etc.

Two Languages

Some people see an agreement as real, as compared to alien, when it is in their own language. This is especially true cross-culturally. Putting agreements in both languages helps avoid interpretation

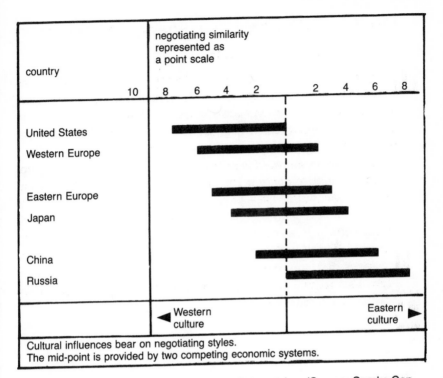

Figure 14-3. Cultural override on negotiating styles. (Source: Sparks Consultants.)

difficulties later. It strengthens the agreement because of the complementary effect on the other party. Dual language clearly indicates recognition of and respect for the other party. It conveys acceptance as an equal. At the same time, it must be clear which language governs the agreement, as translation may alter intent. Figure 14-3 broadly compares negotiating styles based on different cultures.

Dealing with Opponent Styles, Strategies, and Tactics: Summary

Opponents have a primary negotiating style and usually one, sometimes two, secondary styles. Negotiators must balance style accommodations with opponents against their own style selection for each issue. Concurrently, negotiators must retain an overall issue orientation. Negotiators need to develop diagnostic capabilities regarding opponent need orientations and likely tactics. They must be able to initiate confrontation on issues without attacking or demeaning opponents. They should avoid actions that lead opponents to defensiveness or other behavior that retards expeditious resolution and agreement. They continually work at maintaining a high credibility, consisting of both motive and value. They must convey precise messages and preserve appeal so that opponent receptivity stays high. This requires blending information to achieve the perception desired. They must also be good listeners.

Conclusion

Research, planning, and preparation are only valuable when skill, discipline, and patience are available to employ them during negotiations. The negotiator must develop enthusiasm for his position coupled with conviction: this is vital to a negotiator's chances of success.

Haste makes waste.
Benjamin Franklin

Appendix

Checklists

Negotiating is a complex process. Any such process can be helped along by using formatted methods such as checklists. These ensure that the correct number and kinds of things that must be done are not overlooked. The examples provided are intended to stimulate thought as to the aids the negotiator might design. They are primarily for the sale of a product or service. They do not represent the ultimate forms or the variety of applications in different type negotiations, i.e. with governmental agencies or unions, in real estate, for loans, and in acquisition or divestiture and for professional services.

For opponent:
1. What is its industry position regarding
    a. Market share
    b. Technical competence
    c. Financial strength/profitability
    d. Management
2. What is opponent reputation? (include source of data)
3. What is the record with opponent? Past relations and performance regarding
    a. Service
    b. Quality
    c. Cooperation
    d. Flexibility
    e. Reliability
    f. Limitations
4. What future relationship do we want with this opponent?
    a. Short term
    b. Long term

For negotiator:
1. What are structural considerations?
    a. Style we should attempt
    b. Authority we will have
    c. Timing we must meet/schedule compliance
    d. Location we prefer
    e. People who will represent us (names/skills)
2. What are the issues?
    a. Major: strengths/weaknesses
    b. Minor: strengths/weaknesses
3. What is our starting position?
    a. Strategy
    b. Tactics

Figure A-1. Checklist for reviewing key areas prior to analyzing issues.

Goals and objectives
1. Scope: description of work to be done.
2. Specification: standards.
3. Schedule requirements.
4. Conditions:
   a. Risks
   b. Liabilities
   c. Warranties
   d. Concessions
   e. Special clearances
5. Price range: internal cost analysis and projection.

Priorities set
1. Facts determined, separated from assumptions.
2. Matrix prepared.
3. "Must list" made.
4. Secondary issues clarified.
5. Agenda developed.

Strategic considerations
1. Type of contract:
   a. Fixed price
   b. Cost plus
   c. Other
2. Bargaining position:
   a. Urgency
   b. Market conditions
   c. Local constraints
3. Research on opponent.
4. Estimated opponent needs/ wants/ options.
5. Selected setting.
6. Opening position identified.

Team composition
1. Establish roles.
2. Explain control procedures.

Figure A-2. Position checklist.

1. Are we compartmentalized? (Gives opponent advantage of working against nonunified group.)
2. Do we have a pattern? (Opponent can design a strategy to better us.)
3. Do we keep commerical (money) separate from technical (capability) considerations?
4. Do we assess past record of opponent/follow-up?
5. Is our expertise ample (to keep power balanced)?
6. Are we overgenerous because of our size?
7. Are we comfortable in severe conflict situations?
8. Have our "must lists" been satisfactory?
9. Are we patient enough with opponents who are slow to see larger aspects of an issue?
10. Are our communications concise?
11. Do we maintain quid pro quo regarding concessions?
12. Do we avoid suboptimizing within? (Can the opponent determine which area is dominant and play to its needs?)
13. Are our agreement format and terms clear in meaning?
14. Do we allow opponent enough time to present his side? (Do we hurry to the center of things and miss important opponent data?)
15. Are our team members disciplined?
16. Do we establish ranges that have proved to be realistic?
17. Do we adequately use recesses, avoid impulse control and overinvolvement?
18. Are we overbearing and responsible for making negotiations more difficult (i.e. change opponent style or provide him a rationale for being uncooperative)?

Figure A-3. Checklist for identifying weakness due to internal shortcomings.

1. Ambiguous statements and clauses?
    Examples:
    What would be considered *reasonable* to both parties?
    Under *Emergency* conditions, one party will provide or expects to receive what?
2. Specifications. Are they precise?
    Examples:
    Do both parties have the same data for the original agreement?
    Have agreed-to changes been noted in their records by both parties?
3. Time and rates. Are terms precise?
    Examples:
    Is *week* defined by days or hours?
    Is the number of hours in a day defined?
    Is it clear when overtime starts, and what constitutes it?
    Is travel time allowance specified?
    Is travel time paid; at what rate?
4. Are terms tight or loose?
    Examples:
    Are initials used when words should be written out?
    Are acknowledgments specified by time?
5. Shopping list contracts:
    Are usages verified?
    Are general service type contracts backed by verified usage amounts?
6. Escalation clauses. Are they specific?
    Examples:
    Are terms set out for interest by amount and type (compound or simple)?
    Can delivery slippage give opponent an advantage due to escalation clause wording?
    Are penalty clauses ambiguous?

Figure A-4. Checklist for identifying pitfalls in terms and conditions.

Items	Contribution to Outcome				
	4	3	2	1	N/A

Startup
  1. Environment:
     physical setting, amenities.
  2. Projected image:
     where authority lies.
  3. Agenda:
     reviewed, altered.					

Negotiation sessions
  1. Understanding agreement
     terms/conditions.
  2. Opponent:
     performance, capabilities.
  3. Communications:
     clear, effective.
  4. Closure techniques:
     items tacked down.
  5. Goals:
     Could performance have been
     better? Can agreement be
     administered? Were economics
     in line?					

Critique
  1. Was preparation adequate? Strong
     and weak points.
  2. Was team effective?
  3. Were individuals effective?					

Summary
  1. Conclusions:
     recommendations reached;
     goals reached.
  2. Wins:
     How were gains made?
     where did things work out poorly?					

4 = Excellent 1 = poor Totals					

Figure A-5. Evaluating negotiations.

Contractor/vendor _____ File # _____
Address _____ Date _____
Scope of work/job title

Duration of agreement _____ yr _____ mo _____ wk
Agreement # _____ Value ($) _____
Rating ☐ pre ☐ post ☐ combined (✔ one box only)

Description	Good	Satisfactory	Poor	Not rated
1. Labor adequacy				
2. Supervision qualification				
3. (a) Safety compliance (b) Understood job/ performance requirements.				
4. Schedule adherence				
5. Cooperation				
6. Overall performance				
7. Other (describe)				
8.				
9.				

Additional work

Disputes

Remarks

Discussed with contractor/vendor ☐ yes Date _____ ☐ no
Contractor comments

Originator's signature _____

Figure A-6. Evaluating contractor/vendor performance.

Description _____ Reference # _____
Our estimate pre-negotiation $ _____ Date _____
Bid accepted $ _____
Negotiated value $ _____

Our team names   Titles   Departments

Opponents   Titles   Styles

Comments

Issue(s)	Major	Resolved	Minor	Resolved	Stalemate
Ours					
Opponents					

Duration of Negotiation

Recommended future improvements: specific points that will improve our performance in the near term.

Signature/Title >

Figure A-7. Evaluation/critique: negotiation performance.

Bibliography

There are many excellent books that describe the use of negotiating techniques in various situations. The books listed provide a deeper understanding of what happens when these techniques are used.

Berne, Eric, *Games People Play*. N. Y.: Grove Press, 1964.

Chapman, A. H., *Put Offs & Come Ons*. N. Y.: G. P. Putnam's Sons, 1968.

Cooper, Gary L. (ed.), *Theories of Group Process*. N. Y.: John Wiley and Sons, 1975.

Collins, Larry, and Lapierre Dominique, *Freedom at Midnight*. N. Y.: Simon & Schuster, 1975.

Delbecq, A. L., A. H. Van de Ven and D. H. Gustafson, *Group Techniques for Program Planning*. Glenview: Scott Foresman & Co., 1975.

Franklin, Benjamin, *Poor Richard's Almanacs* (1733-1758). N. Y.: George Macy Companies, 1964.

Hovland, J. K., *Psychology of Communication and Persuasion*. New Haven: Yale Press.

Jepson, R. W., *Clear Thinking*. London: Longmans, Green & Co., 1955.

Jay, Anthony, *Management And Machiavelli*. N. Y.: Holt, Rinehart and Winston, 1967.

Ibid. *The New Oratory*. N. Y: American Management Association, 1971.

Lee, Irving, *How to Talk with People*. N. Y.: Harper, 1952.

Rapoport, Anatol, *Flights, Games and Debates*. Ann Arbor: The University of Michigan, 1966.

Schoenburn, David, *Triumph In Paris*. N. Y.: Harper & Row, 1976.

Stebbing, L. S., *Thinking to Some Purpose*. N. Y.: Penguin Books, 1959.

Schwartz, Tony, *The Responsive Chord*. Garden City: Anchor Books, 1973.

Williams, Frederick, *Reasoning With Statistics*. N.Y.: Holt, Rinehart & Winston, 1978.

Index